# 81 Fresh & Fun Critical-Thinking Activities

**Engaging Activities and Reproducibles to Develop Kids' Higher-Level Thinking Skills**

by Laurie Rozakis

SCHOLASTIC
PROFESSIONAL BOOKS

New York ★ Toronto ★ London ★ Aukland ★ Sydney

# Dedication

· · · · · · · · · · · · · ·

With love and thanks, I dedicate this book to all the fine teachers who have enriched my life: Barbara Bengels, Chris LaRosa, Ed Leigh, Jack McGrath, Jim Pepperman, Jennifer Richmond, Elizabeth Simmons, Lenore Strober, and Tom Thibadeau.

Cover design by Jaime Lucero
Interior design by Jaime Lucero and Robert Dominguez for Grafica, Inc.
Interior illustrations by Maxie Chambliss

ISBN: 0-590-37526-1

# Contents

# Introduction

Today's students will inherit a complex and rapidly changing world, a world in which they'll be required to absorb new ideas, examine and interpret information, apply knowledge, and solve unconventional problems. To deal with the information explosion of the twenty-first century, students will need to develop systematic ways of thinking and reasoning. Critical-thinking skills will be essential.

What is *critical thinking*? It's the ability to:

- **solve problems**
- **make products that are valued in a particular culture**
- **be flexible, creative, and original**
- **think about thinking**
- **locate the appropriate route to a goal**
- **capture and transmit knowledge**
- **express views and feelings appropriately**

Effective critical thinkers use one or more of the seven multiple intelligences identified by Dr. Howard Gardner:

1. **verbal/linguistic**
2. **logical/mathematical**
3. **visual/spatial**
4. **bodily/kinesthetic**
5. **musical/rhythmic**
6. **interpersonal (the ability to work cooperatively in a group)**
7. **intrapersonal (self-identity)**

Research indicates that critical thinking is neither inborn nor naturally acquired. In fact, fewer than half the adults in America today have the ability to reflect upon their thinking and explain how they solved a problem.

Fortunately, critical thinking *can* be taught and learned. This book, and its companion volume for younger grades, will help you teach students to reflect upon their own thinking processes and become more successful, active learners. Both professional educators and parents can use this book to help children learn to think critically.

In our daily lives, we use many critical-thinking skills simultaneously—and not in any prescribed order. For the purposes of this book, however, the critical-thinking activities are arranged in a hierarchy, beginning with the skills of recognition and recall and working up to the more advanced skills of analysis and synthesis. This arrangement will help you and your students more clearly understand and identify the specific critical-thinking skills they are using.

For each thinking skill in this book, there are two kinds of activities: (1) those that you, as the teacher, will lead, and (2) student reproducibles for independent work. On the introductory pages for each section of the book, you'll find ideas for introducing and using the student reproducibles. You can use the Try This! activity at the bottom of each reproducible as an extension of the lesson, a challenge activity, or a homework assignment.

Here are some ways you can use the lessons to help students become more effective thinkers:

1. **Read each activity aloud or have a child read it aloud to the rest of the group.**
2. **Allow children ample time to think and respond.**
3. **Ask students questions to assess their understanding of the problem.**
4. **Welcome different strategies for solving the problem. Encourage divergent thinking.**
5. **Observe children as they work in order monitor their problem-solving skills.**
6. **Give helpful hints to those children who are having difficulty finding ways to approach the problem.**
7. **Guide children to link the problem to others they have already solved.**
8. **Encourage children to check their work.**
9. **Help children explore their thinking and identify the strategies that worked—and those that didn't.**
10. **Invite students to share their results.**

Since critical thinking doesn't end when an individual project does, you will want to give students sufficient time to evaluate their thinking strategies. Guide students to formulate ways they might adjust their critical-thinking strategies with the next problems they solve.

Finally, model critical thinking for students by sharing your own problem-solving strategies and accepting unusual and unexpected strategies and solutions. Your participation as an active learner will further reinforce the critical-thinking skills you teach.

Above all, encourage your students to see themselves as thinkers.

# Recognizing and Recalling Activities

To begin thinking critically, students must first learn to recognize and recall key information. These skills are important for the mastery of higher-level skills such as classification, inferring, and analyzing.

The activities in this section will help students tap their prior knowledge to identify and remember key facts. You can present each of the following activities as a complete lesson or integrate the activities into lessons in different curriculum areas. The section begins with the easier activities and concludes with more difficult ones. Instructions for teacher-led activities appear on the same page as the activity. Use the teacher notes that follow for the student reproducibles.

## Cross-Curricular Links

| Activity | Page | Content Area |
|---|---|---|
| Time Capsule | 8 | language arts |
| Mind Squeeze | 9 | language arts |
| Trivia Trackdown | 10 | math, science/social studies |
| Wordplay | 11 | language arts |
| Making a Menu | 12 | science/health |
| Recycled Words | 13 | language arts |
| What Am I? | 14 | language arts/science/social studies |
| Arctic Facts | 15 | science/social studies |
| Antarctic Facts | 16 | science/social studies |
| What's Up & What's Down? | 17–18 | science/social studies |
| Transformations | 19 | mathematics |

## Teacher Notes for Student Reproducibles

### Page 9: Mind Squeeze
This activity tests students' observation and memory skills. After the class completes the reproducible, discuss various strategies that students used to recall the items on the page. For example, they might have memorized them in rows or columns; they might have classified them into groups.

### Page 10: Trivia Trackdown
Trivia Trackdown is a great way to sharpen students' recognition and recalling skills. You might begin by having students complete this page independently or with a partner. Then have the class research general information on science,

art, music, literature, sports, geography, history, and other subjects. Students can write questions on index cards with the answers on the back. Collect the cards and divide the class into teams. Have the teams line up on different sides of the room and take turns answering the questions as you call them out. Award points for correctly answered questions.

**Page 11: Wordplay**
Before students begin this page, you might want to review the parts of speech—noun, pronouns and verbs—essential to a sentence. Invite students to read their word lists and paragraphs aloud to the class.

**Page 12: Making a Menu**
You may wish to have students work with partners to complete this page. Encourage the teams to share their "menus" with the class.

**Page 13: Recycled Words**
Before assigning this page, review what students know about open and closed compound words. Point out that compound words can also be proper nouns.

**Page 14: What Am I?**
After students complete the page, work with the class to come up with more definitions for other words beginning with *h.* Students might also enjoy acting out some of their definitions.

**Page 15: Arctic Facts**
This page helps students recognize, recall, and organize facts. It also gives them practice in extrapolating important information from a passage. Encourage students to paraphrase the information they include in the web.

**Page 16: Antarctic Facts**
This page is similar to page 15. Completing the web will help students recognize, recall, and organize facts from a nonfiction passage. Discuss with the class why these are important skills.

**Pages 17–18: What's Up and What's Down?**
Students will need to review the information on pages 15 and 16 before playing this game with a partner. Encourage the teams to make up additional questions for others to answer.

**Page 19: Transformations**
This page calls for students to use shape, size, and color to identify a pattern. You may wish to complete the first item with the class to be sure students understand what they are expected to do.

# Time Capsule

**Here's a unique way to use literature to help your students recognize and gather key ideas. Begin by selecting a novel or short story that the entire class has read fairly recently. Write the title and the name of the main character on the chalkboard. Then ask students to list six to ten items from the book that were important to the main character. This can be done individually or in small groups. If the students read Gary Paulsen's _Hatchet_, for example, the list might look like this:**

hatchet
bow and arrow
airplane
cave
fire
lake
fish
emergency transmitter
raspberries

Next, ask students to put themselves in the main character's place. As the main character, which of these items might they want to save in a time capsule? What other items might they add? Have each student create a short list of things they would put in a time capsule for the main character. Students should be able to explain their choices.

You can expand this activity by having students make real time capsules for characters in other books and stories or for themselves. What items might best express other characters' personalities—or their own? What items best capture the fictional or real experience? You might want to create a class time capsule. Ask each student to contribute one item. Then bury the capsule somewhere on the school grounds.

**Name** _____

# Mind Squeeze
● ● ● ● ● ● ● ● ● ● ● ● ● ● ● ● ● ● ●

**Take two minutes to look at the words and objects on this page. Then turn the page over and see how many you can recall. Good luck!**

HOMEWORK

STUDY!

SUMMER VACATION

GOOD!

SUNGLASSES

RAINBOW

LUNCH

**Try This!** **Do It Again** Repeat the activity. Can you improve your performance?

9

Name _____

# Trivia Trackdown

**How many of these questions can you answer?**

**1.** How many squares are there on a checkerboard?

**2.** What is the name of Mickey Mouse's dog?

**3.** What kind of animal is Babar?

**4.** What was the name of the Wright Brothers' airplane?

**5.** What is the capital of New York?

**6.** What do frogs have in their mouths that toads don't?

**7.** Who was the first woman to sit on the Supreme Court?

**8.** What nations border the continental U.S. on the north and south?

**9.** Who created *The Cat in the Hat*?

**10.** How many queen bees are in each hive?

**11.** Who was the second president of the United States?

**12.** How many teaspoons make up a tablespoon?

**13.** What two states share Kansas City?

**14.** Who is the Friendly Ghost?

**15.** Name the Great Lakes.

**16.** Who painted the "Mona Lisa"?

**17.** What substance inside corn makes it pop?

**18.** How many sides are there on a snowflake?

**19.** How many wings does a bee have?

**20.** How many pints are in a quart?

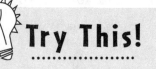 **Try This!** **Think of Another** Think of another trivia question for a classmate to answer.

# Wordplay

Imagine you live in a world with only 20 words. You can use these 20 words as much as you want, but you cannot use any other words at all. In the space below, list the 20 words you'd pick:

1. _____
2. _____
3. _____
4. _____
5. _____
6. _____
7. _____
8. _____
9. _____
10. _____

11. _____
12. _____
13. _____
14. _____
15. _____
16. _____
17. _____
18. _____
19. _____
20. _____

 **Try This!**

**Use Your Words** Now, write a paragraph using *only* your 20 words! Make sure your paragraph has at least five sentences.

# Making a Menu

It's dinner time, but what are you going to eat? Complete this page to help you think of a menu.

**Food that begins with _b_:**

1. _____
2. _____
3. _____
4. _____
5. _____

**Food that grows below ground:**

1. _____
2. _____
3. _____
4. _____
5. _____

**Fast food:**

1. _____
2. _____
3. _____
4. _____
5. _____

**Food that grows on trees:**

1. _____
2. _____
3. _____
4. _____
5. _____

**Food that is white:**

1. _____
2. _____
3. _____
4. _____
5. _____

**Now, list your five favorite foods:**

1. _____
2. _____
3. _____
4. _____
5. _____

 **Try This!** **Favorite Foods** Make a graph showing the five favorite foods of your classmates.

# Recycled Words

You probably recycle cans and newspapers, but did you know that you can recycle words too? You can use the same word to make many different words and phrases. For example, you might use the word ice to make the words ice skate, iceberg or ice water.

**For each row, add the same word on the lines to make new words.**

**Example:** *coat* check     *coat* room     *coat* of arms

1. _____ lash     _____ brow     _____ sight

2. _____ mark     _____ mine     _____ scape

3. _____ born     _____ England     _____ Year's Day

4. _____ work     _____ test     _____ block

5. _____ around     _____ away     _____ off

6. _____ shape     _____ wreck     _____ yard

7. _____ bow     _____ coat     _____ dance

8. _____ storm     _____ plow     _____ shoe

9. _____ pen     _____ house     _____ room

10. _____ roll     _____ shell     _____ nog

**Try This!**    **Use the Words** Use the words that you made in sentences.

# What Am I?
· · · · · · · · · · · · · · · ·

**Below is a list of definitions for words that begin with the letter h.
See how many you can guess.**

**Words That Start with *h***

1.  Balls of ice that fall from the sky                     _____

2.  A 17-syllable Japanese poem                            _____

3.  Not whole                                              _____

4.  A patty of chopped beef                                _____

5.  An allergy to grasses and weeds                        _____

6.  The organ that pumps blood                             _____

7.  A great person; someone people admire                 _____

8.  Opposite of *low*                                      _____

9.  The study of past events                               _____

10. A country known for its tulips                         _____

**Try This!**  **Define It**  Write a definition for each of these *h* words: *hello, handkerchief, horse.*

# Arctic Facts

**Read the passage about the Arctic. Then fill in the web with facts from the passage. Include at least three facts for each heading.**

The Arctic is a large region of the earth around the North Pole. This region includes the Arctic Ocean, Greenland, Iceland, thousands of smaller islands, and the northern parts of three continents: North America, Europe, and Asia. Many of the inhabitants are Eskimos, people native to the region. Still others are Lapps, Yakuts, and Chukchi.

Wildlife in the Arctic includes wolves, polar bears, foxes, many birds, caribou, lemmings, voles, walrus, and Arctic hares. The most common Arctic fish is the char, a kind of trout.

The Arctic climate is harsh. Temperatures can reach 70 degrees below freezing in the winter. Blustering winds make the weather even more bitter. Summers are short and cool.

**People**
1. _____
2. _____
3. _____

**Location**
1. _____
2. _____
3. _____

**ARCTIC**

**Animals**
1. _____
2. _____
3. _____

**Climate**
1. _____
2. _____
3. _____

 **Try This!** **Add More** Add another circle to the web. Label it "Plants". Then find three facts to put in the circle.

# Antarctic Facts

**Read the passage about the Antarctic. Then fill in the web with facts from the passage. Include at least three facts for each heading.**

Antarctica is the continent at the South Pole. Antarctica is surrounded by three oceans—the Atlantic, Pacific, and Indian. It is the fifth largest continent and the coldest place on Earth. Because it is below the equator, winter in Antarctica takes place when it is summer in the United States. Metal shatters like glass in the brutal Antarctic winter. Temperatures drop to 120 below zero; a person without the right clothing would freeze solid in just a few minutes. Winds gusting up to 200 miles per hour come screaming down the ice, tearing into the piles of snow.

With the exception of a few insects, Antarctica has no animal life on its land. However, penguins, seals, whales, krill, and seabirds thrive in the oceans around the continent. Likewise, few plants besides mosses grow on the ice-covered land of Antarctica.

No people live permanently on this continent, but Antarctica is known for its scientific stations. Many nations, including the U.S., Chile, Norway, Great Britain, and Australia have large research centers where scientists study earthquakes, gravity, oceans, and weather conditions.

**Location**
1. _____
2. _____
3. _____

**Climate**
1. _____
2. _____
3. _____

**ANTARCTIC**

**Wildlife**
1. _____
2. _____
3. _____

**Science**
1. _____
2. _____
3. _____

 **Try This!** **Learn More** Find out about the first people to explore Antarctica. Add another circle to the web to show what you learned.

Name _____

# What's Up and What's Down?

**See how much you learned about the Arctic and Antarctic by playing this game with a partner. Here's how:**

**1.** Cut apart the cards, shuffle them, and place them in a stack facing down.
**2.** Take turns picking a card and asking your partner a question.
**3.** If their answer is correct, pick another card and ask another question. If they answer incorrectly, they pick a card and ask you a question.
**4.** The player who answers the most questions correctly wins.

What continent is the South Pole on?

[Antarctica]

What is the coldest place on the earth?

[the South Pole, Antarctica]

Who lives at the North Pole today?

[mostly Eskimos, Yakuts, Lapps, Chukchi]

What large birds live near Antartica?

[penguins]

At which Pole can you find wolves, foxes, and polar bears?

[the North Pole]

Who lives at the South Pole today?

[Visiting scientists only.]

 **Try This!**

**Find More** Use a book to find more animals that you can add to this page.

17

**What kinds of plants grow at the South Pole?**

[mostly mosses]

**What is a char?**

[a kind of trout]

**In what region of the earth would you find Greenland?**

[Arctic]

**What oceans surround Antarctica?**

[Indian, Pacific, Atlantic]

**In which region would you expect to find temperatures 120 degrees below zero?**

[Antarctic]

**Which region includes parts of other continets?**

[Arctic]

**What do scientists study on Antarctica?**

[earthquakes, weather conditions, gravity, oceans]

**What animals live permanently on Antarctica's land?**

[none, only insects]

**What is the fifth largest continent?**

[Antarctica]

**Try This!** **Write a Question** Make up a question of your own about the Arctic or Antarctic. Have your partner answer it.

# Transformations

Study the first pair of shapes in each example. Think about how A changes into B. Then look at C. Which of the six numbered shapes changes in relation to C in the same way that A changes to B? Find that shape. Circle the number of your answer.

1.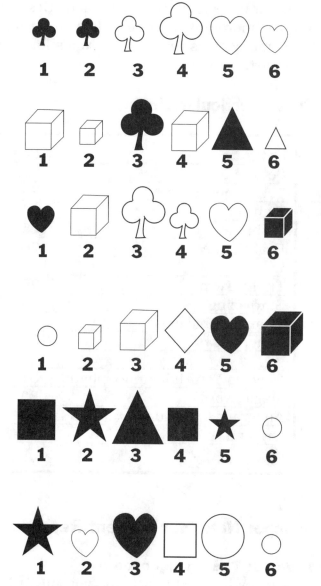

2.

3.

4.

5.

6.

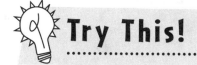 **Try This!**   **Explain** Write a sentence or two to tell why you chose the answer you did.

19

# Distinguishing and Visualizing Activities

When students become skilled at distinguishing between important and unimportant data and visualizing problem-solving strategies, they naturally develop more logical and effective patterns of thinking. The activities in this section will help students learn to identify specific items and form strong mental images.

Use the chart to help you relate the activities in this section to your class curriculum. In general, the easier activities appear at the beginning of the section, and the more difficult ones follow. Instructions for teacher-led activities are on the same page as the activity. Notes for using the student reproducibles follow the chart.

## Cross-Curricular Links

| Activity | Page | Content Area |
| --- | --- | --- |
| Set the Scene | 22 | art/language arts |
| The Qqqqqooooo | 23 | art/language arts |
| Tight Fit | 24 | art/mathematics |
| Within a Word | 25 | language arts |
| Real Estate | 26 | social studies/ mathematics |
| Tricky Twins | 27 | art/mathematics |
| Stargazing | 28 | science |
| Triangle Challenge | 29 | mathematics |
| Tangrams | 30 | math/multicultural/ art |
| How Do You Hide an Elephant? | 31 | language arts |
| Magic Words | 32 | language arts |
| Anagram Adventure | 33 | language arts |
| Origami | 34–35 | multicultural/art |

## Teacher Notes for Student Reproducibles

### Page 23: The Qqqqqooooo
As a follow-up to this activity, you might have students write a story about the creature they create. Invite students to share their artwork and stories with the class.

**Page 25: Within a Word**

In this activity, students must visualize the word *bar* in other, longer words. Follow up by having students write a sentence using each of the words they identify.

**Page 26: Real Estate**

Before students complete this page, you might want to discuss the term *real estate* to make sure everyone knows what it means. Follow up by talking about the variety of homes pictured and how and why homes differ around the world.

**Page 27: Tricky Twins**

To further enhance students' visual skills, have them describe each pair of cats that they identify.

**Page 28: Stargazing**

Follow up by having students find at least one fact about each of the names on the puzzle.

**Page 29: Triangle Challenge**

Before students begin working on the page, have them identify the kind of triangle they see (equilateral). What other kinds of triangles can students name? What other geometrical shapes?

**Page 30: Tangrams**

Have students identify the geometrical shapes that make up the seven tangram pieces. Create a bulletin board display with the tangram pictures students make.

**Page 31: How Do You Hide an Elephant?**

Point out to students that they can use the hidden word idea as a code. Challenge them to write coded messages.

**Page 32: Magic Words**

In this activity, students must visualize and rearrange letters into different word configurations. Challenge students to use the new words in complete sentences.

**Page 33: Anagram Adventure**

This page builds on the activity on page 32. However, students are now asked to rearrange letters to create more than one word. Again, encourage students to use the words they create in complete sentences.

# Set the Scene

**One way to enhance student's visualization skills is to have them create dioramas or other three-dimensional representations of specific scenes from literature. Ask students to bring in shoe boxes. Begin the activity by reviewing the stories, poems, novels, and plays the class has read during the year. Discuss scenes that are especially dramatic. List some of these scenes on the chalkboard.**

Then invite students to select a scene to bring to life. They may want to sketch the scene on a piece of paper before transforming it into three-dimensional form. Students can use construction paper and small objects such as pebbles, sticks, and blocks in their scenes. Encourage them to experiment with depth and space by placing figures and objects in the background, middle ground, and foreground of their scenes. Students can use strips of fanned paper to anchor the figures and objects.

Glue here to position on wall.

Glue folded strip to cut-out figure along here.

Glue here to position on floor.

Back of cut-out princess

Name _____

# The Qqqqqooooo

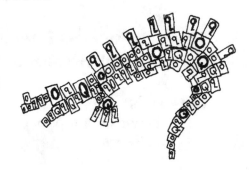

What's a Qqqqqooooo? It's a make-believe creature made from letters. Make a letter creature of your own. It can be a real animal or a make-believe one.

## Here's what you'll need:

old newspapers or magazines
pen or pencil
glue

scissors
construction paper

## Here's what to do:

**1.** Pick any two letters.

**2.** Cut a pile of these letters from old newspapers or magazines.

**3.** Put the letters together to make a creature. When you like the way they look, glue the letters down in the frame on this page.

 **Try This!** **Introduce Your Creature** Give your creature a name and write a brief description of it, including where it lives, what it eats, and what makes it special.

23

# Tight Fit

**This activity is an interesting way for students to practice distinguishing and visualizing both positive and negative space.**

## Materials:

construction paper       crayons
scissors

## Directions:

1. Arrange students in small groups of four or five. Give each group a stack of paper, some crayons, and a pair of scissors per student.

2. Have each student fold one sheet of paper in half and draw a geometric design along the folded edge. Caution students not to copy each other's drawings.

3. Then have students cut out their shapes along the fold so that they have two pieces of paper—the shape and the leftover paper.

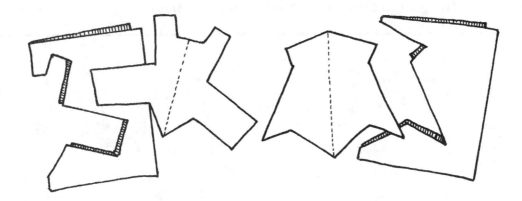

4. Have each group select a member to collect all the cut-out shapes. This person becomes the first player.

5. The rest of the group makes a circle around the player and displays one of the cut papers, unfolded.

6. The player must try to visualize which "negative" each cut-out "positive" fits and then place the shape in the open space.

7. When the player has correctly fit each shape to its template, have each group select a new player and repeat the round.

8. After two or three rounds, invite groups to exchange their cut-outs and negatives and continue playing.

Name _____

# Within a Word

Can you find the word *bar* in the word for each of these pictures? Write the word on the line.

1. 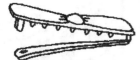 _____

2. 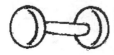 _____

3.  _____

4.  _____

5.  _____

6.  _____

7.  _____

8.  _____

9. 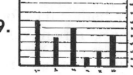 _____

**Try This!** **Find More** Think of at least three more words with *bar* in them.

25

# Real Estate
· · · · · · · · · · · · · · · ·

**Look carefully at the homes on this page. Then answer the questions.**

1. How many homes have only two windows and one door?

2. How many homes have no windows?

3. How many homes are not for people?

4. How many homes do not have walls made of wood?

5. How many homes float?

6. How many homes have flags flying?

7. How many homes have 12 or more windows?

8. How many homes have a porch?

 **Try This!** **Draw**  Draw a picture of
· · · · · · · · · · · · · another home. Then reread
the questions. How do the answers change?

# Tricky Twins

The cats are having a party. Most of the cats are twins dressed just alike and standing the same way, but three single cats are at the party, too. With a colored pen or pencil, find and number the 12 pairs of identical twins. Then circle the three cats that have no twin.

💡 **Try This!** **Draw**   Choose one of the single cats. Draw a twin for that cat.

# Stargazing

It's time to study the skies, but you won't need a telescope! Why? Because some stellar things are hidden in this puzzle. Find each of the heavenly bodies listed below. The words go across, down, and backwards.

**Find these words:**

| Orion | Saturn | Earth | North Star | Moon |
|-------|--------|-------|------------|------|
| Sun | Milky Way | Mars | Venus | Pluto |

```
M N O R T H S T A R
I C R S W R U M N J
L H I S Y U U S E A
K A O T U L P A A Z
Y R N O O M O T R U
W L Q U A A Y U T Z
A E L O B R O R H O
Y S P W B S U N E V
```

**Try This!** **Classify** Look at the names you found. Think of a way to classify them into groups.

**Name** _____

# Triangle Challenge

**How many triangles can you find in this shape? Use colored pencils to outline each triangle. Write your total in the space below.**

There are _____ triangles.

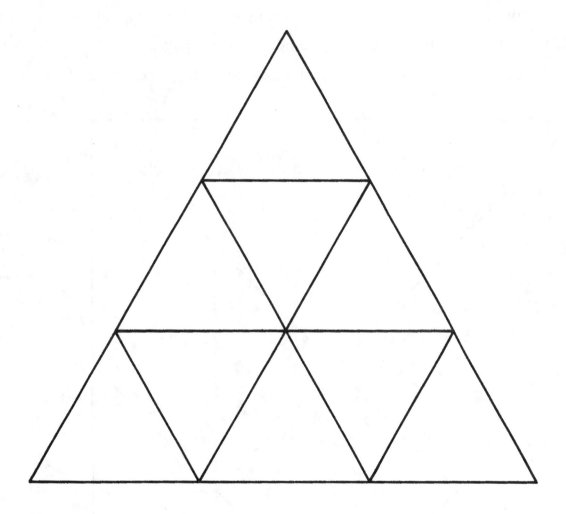

 **Try This!** **Look Again** Remove one line from the shape. Now how many triangles are there?

# Tangrams

A tangram is a Chinese puzzle made from a square cut into seven pieces—5 triangles, 1 square, and 1 rhomboid. You can use tangram pieces to make different figures. Here's how:

**1.** Cut out the square.

**2.** Cut on the lines to make the five triangles, one square, and one rhomboid.

**3.** Arrange the shapes to make the figure on this page.

**4.** Now make your own tangram pictures. Glue the pieces in place for the picture you like the best.

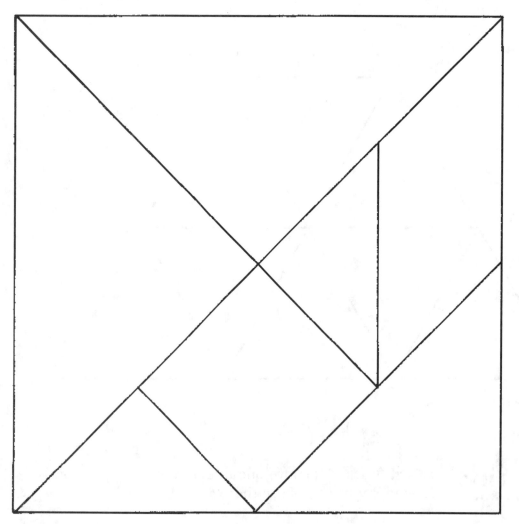

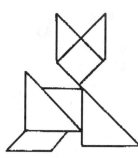

 **Try This!**   **Make More**  Use all seven tangram pieces to make a vehicle.

# How Do You Hide an Elephant?

You probably can't hide an elephant in your room, but you can hide one in a sentence. Let's start small. Can you find the goat that is hiding in the sentence below?

Lisa will go at dinner time.

The two words *go at* spell goat when you put them together.

Now, find these animals in the sentences below. Underline the letters that spell the animal names.

| | | | |
|---|---|---|---|
| ape | deer | horse | rat |
| kitten | owl | dog | bear |
| lamb | hen | pony | mice |

1. Go fish or see what we have to eat in the refrigerator.

2. Be artistic and paint a picture for me.

3. She needs a new cover for her book.

4. Tom iced the cake for the birthday party.

5. Do girls like soccer or baseball?

6. Ms. Dee read a book to the class.

7. What a big bowl of noodles you have!

8. Hop on your bicycle and let's go for a ride.

9. Jess took a peek into the package.

10. "Slam bam!" the ball hit the rim with a crash!

11. Jay did kick it ten times in row.

12. Please have dinner at my house on Monday.

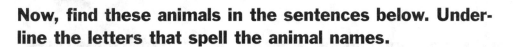

**Try This!** **Don't Forget the Elephant** Now about that elephant. Write a sentence that hides an elephant. Then switch papers with a friend and see if you can find one another's elephants.

31

# Magic Words

Sometimes a word is just a word. But other times, words can be magic! Just move letters around and you have new words. Take a look at the examples below:

| Original Word | New Word |
| --- | --- |
| on | no |
| now | won |
| pot | top |
| bat | tab |

**See if you can rearrange the underlined words below to match the clues.**

1. Change <u>sore</u> to a thorny flower.　　　　　　_____

2. Change <u>bus</u> to a type of underwater transportation.　　_____

3. Change <u>add</u> to a word for *father*.　　　　　　_____

4. Change <u>not</u> to a word for 2,000 pounds.　　　　_____

5. Change <u>stone</u> to little messages.　　　　　　_____

6. Change <u>panel</u> to a flying machine.　　　　　　_____

7. Change <u>net</u> to the number of fingers and toes you have.　_____

8. Change <u>low</u> to a very wise bird.　　　　　　_____

9. Change <u>raw</u> to a word for battle.　　　　　　_____

10. Change <u>sale</u> to an animal.　　　　　　　　_____

**Try This!**　**More Magic**　What other magic words can you think of? Write some in the box below.

# Anagram Adventure

An anagram is a word that is made by rearranging the letters of another word. For example, here are four anagrams from the word post:

| stop | pots | tops | spot |

Can you form at least two anagrams from each of these words?

**1. dare**

_____

_____

**2. teas**

_____

_____

**3. meat**

_____

_____

**4. pear**

_____

_____

**5. stale**

_____

_____

**6. pans**

_____

_____

**7. snail**

_____

_____

**8. acre**

_____

_____

**9. slap**

_____

_____

 **Try This!** **More Anagrams** See if you can form a third anagram for three of the words above.

33

# Origami

**A great way to build visualization skills is by introducing students to the Japanese art of paper folding, origami.**

**Give students these step-by-step instructions for creating an origami rabbit:**

**1.** Label points on the sides of a square with the letters A–H as shown. Be sure to write the letters on both sides of the paper.

**2.** Fold the square in half vertically (G to H). Unfold. Fold in half horizontally (E to F) and unfold. Fold point A to point D, creating diagonal CB. Unfold and fold point B to point C, making the diagonal AD. Unfold. These four folds are "helping" folds, made to crease the paper so that subsequent folds will be easier.

**3.** Fold line AC to line GH and then fold line BD to line GH.

**4.** Fold points A and B down to lie on horizontal line EF.

**5.** Place thumbs inside two corner pockets and pull points A and B outward and down to make triangular points. Place an O at the center of the top line of the figure. (Be sure to check with illustration No. 4.)

**6.** From top point O make diagonal folds to points A and B.

**7.** Fold bottom corners C and D back.

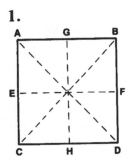

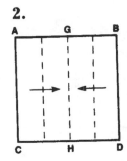

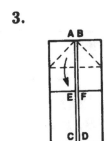

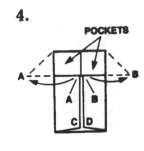

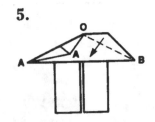

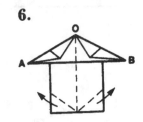

**8.** Fold model in half (reversing centerfold).

**9.** Fold the tail inward (a "squash fold"). Push thumb into point to keep the fold even and pinch the sides together.

*Rabbit is taken from* Papercrafts *by Ian Adair (David and Charles Holdings, Ltd., 1975).*

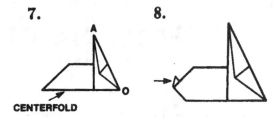

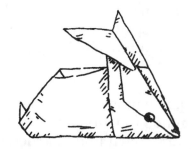

# Activities for Following Directions and Classifying

After students feel comfortable distinguishing and visualizing different aspects of a problem, it is time for them to work on following directions and classifying information. The ability to follow directions helps students work through a process one step at a time. Knowing how to classify information helps them to bring order to a problem by organizing its pieces into groups based on common features.

Consider presenting one or more of these activities at the start of class every day to remind students of the importance of following directions with regard to all their work. You'll find instructions for teacher-led activities on the same page as the activity. Notes for student reproducibles follow the chart on this page. As in the other sections of the book, the easier activities appear first.

As students complete the activities, encourage them to think aloud. This will help you observe the thought processes that they are using.

Use the following chart to help you coordinate the activities with other parts of your curriculum.

## Cross-Curricular Links

| Activity | Page | Content Area |
|---|---|---|
| Quick Draw | 38 | art |
| Wrong Rhymes | 39 | language arts |
| Turn-Around Numbers | 40 | mathematics |
| Are We There Yet? | 41 | social studies |
| Save Yourself! | 42 | social studies |
| Scrambled Sentences | 43 | language arts |
| On the Wild Side, Parts I & II | 44–46 | science |
| Get Set | 47 | mathematics |
| In Groups | 48 | language arts/social studies |
| Prime Time Numbers | 49 | mathematics |

# Teacher Notes for Student Reproducibles

### Page 39: Wrong Rhymes
Before students begin work on this page, you may wish to remind them that some long vowel sounds can be spelled in more than one way. Follow up this activity by challenging students to use one or more sets of the rhymes in a poem.

### Page 41: Are We There Yet?
In this activity, students must write, read, and follow directions. You may wish to have students try out the directions they write before they pass them on to a classmate. Post the finished maps on a bulletin board.

### Page 42: Save Yourself!
If necessary, review the use of a map scale and a compass rose to determine distance and direction.

### Pages 44-46: On the Wild Side, Parts I-II
The activities on these pages call for students to classify information. Tell students that although their classifications may differ slightly, they should be prepared to explain their reasoning.

### Page 47: Get Set
This page gives students experience in identifying different kinds of sets. Remind students to be ready to justify their thinking.

### Page 48: In Groups
In this activity, students must first determine what the group is and then identify the item that does not belong. Students must also explain why that item does not fit the group.

### Page 49: Prime Time Numbers
Ask students to demonstrate why some numbers are not prime numbers.

# Quick Draw

· · · · · · · · · · · · · · · · ·

You can use art as well as numbers to sharpen students' abilities to follow directions. Have each student take out a sheet of paper and a pencil. Explain that you are going to read a series of directions for the class to follow. Then read these directions:

1. Draw a square in the bottom left-hand corner of the paper.

2. Draw another square in the bottom right-hand corner of the paper.

3. Draw a circle in the middle of each square.

4. Put a dot at the center of each circle.

5. Draw a line connecting the two squares.

6. Draw four triangles an inch from the top of the page.

7. Put an X in the first triangle on the right.

8. Draw a circle inside the second triangle from the right.

8. Draw a square inside the circle.

10. Put a square in the third triangle from the right.

11. Color in the last triangle.

12. Draw a circle around that triangle.

13. Draw a line across the middle of the page.

14. Use that line as one side of a rectangle.

15. Write your full name in script in the rectangle.

16. Draw a square directly above the rectangle.

17. Divide the square in half.

18. Color in half of the square.

Have students compare their drawings. Do they all look alike? Discuss which directions could be reworded to be more precise.

# Wrong Rhymes

**Each word group contains three words that rhyme and one that does not. Circle the word that does not rhyme.**

1.  butter, flutter, matter, gutter

2.  got, block, sock, frock

3.  tricked, kicked, lacked, licked

4.  sunny, funny, honey, furry

5.  frail, train, snail, stale

6.  moan, down, tone, groan

7.  kelp, help, talk, yelp

8.  light, blind, hind, find

9.  hate, crate, lake, gate

10. reaky, squeaky, cheery, cheeky

11. dumb, plumb, gum, jump

12. run, plum, sum, hum

13. lace, base, taste, race

14. spill, peel, seal, feel

15. hoot, boat, flute, scoot

16. hair, fair, bear, dead

17. sock, croon, soon, tune

18. sour, sooner, flower, shower

19. type, hike, ripe, pipe

20. sweet, treat, bread, feet

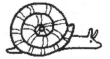

 **Try This!** **Keep Rhyming** Think of another word to rhyme with each group of words.

# Turn-Around Numbers

This number activity challenges students to listen carefully and follow directions. It calls for students to count backward, count forward, and skip lines. Ask students to take out a piece of lined paper. Then give them a series of directions. (You can select any sequence of steps you wish, keeping your students' abilities in mind). Here's an example:

**1.** Write the number 86.                                              (86)

**2.** Count backward five numbers, and write the new number.                                              (81)

**3.** Skip a line, count forward three numbers, skip another line, and write the new number.                                              (84)

**4.** Count backward eight, forward two, skip two lines, write the new number.                                              (78)

**5.** Count forward nine, skip a line, and write the new number.                                              (87)

**6.** Count backward eight, skip a line, count backward six, skip a line, and write the new number.                                              (73)

**7.** Count forward three, skip a line, count forward ten, skip a line, and write the new number.                                              (86)

**8.** Underline the new number. What is it?                                              (<u>86</u>)

**Continue the activity with different numbers and functions!**

# Are We There Yet?

In the space below, write directions from your classroom to any place in the school building, such as the cafeteria, the library, or the gym. Do not write the name of your destination. Instead, write: *And then you are there*. When you have finished writing your mystery directions, exchange papers with a classmate and create a map based on his or her directions. In the space provided, write the name of the destination. Exchange papers with that classmate once again to see if you were right.

**Directions:**

_____

_____

_____

_____

_____

**Map:**

**The destination is:**

 **Try This!**

**Review Your Work** Talk with your partner about ways you could make the directions you wrote and the map that you drew clearer.

# Save Yourself!

Below is a map of the Kingdom of Og, a sad and dangerous land. Unfortunately, you were passing through Og when your camels went into revolt. Now the fierce residents of Og are after you, and your precious cargo of peanut butter—the rarest and most sought-after item in all of Og. Your only chance of survival is to escape to Zog, where peanut-butter is not at all popular. While you may not have your camels, you do have a map to lead you there. Draw your path in pencil; mark each stop with an X. Follow these directions.

### Directions

Go northeast four miles to the mountains. Head four miles due north to the castle, where you'll make a quick stop for lunch. Then travel eight miles northwest to the lake, where you'll take a refreshing dip. Then go 16 miles east to the oasis for a rest. From the oasis, continue east five miles to the bike stand, where you'll hop on a bike and head north to Zog. Good luck!

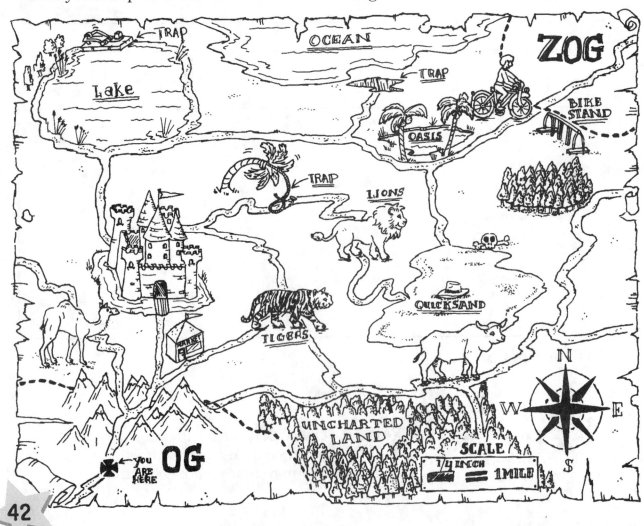

# Scrambled Sentences

**Write this sentence on the board and have students copy it onto a sheet of paper:**

O xwen o my zoct xand O saiz, "Zoct, O broked my arml in hr plaxces."
Hex saiz, "Wellp, tayl xout of th laces."

**Then tell students to follow your directions to unscramble the sentence. Read aloud the following:**

**1.** Change all the *z*'s to *d*'s.

**2.** Cross off all the *x*'s.

**3.** Add a *t* to the end of the second word, the beginning of the third word, and the beginning of the fifteenth word.

**4.** Change the three capital *o*'s to capital *i*'s.

**5.** Add a *p* to the beginning of the last word.

**6.** Cross off the last letter in the eleventh, thirteenth, and nineteenth words.

**7.** Put an *s* on the front of the twentieth word and cross off the last letter.

**8.** Add *or* to the end of the fifth and ninth word.

**9.** Add *ee* to the end of the fifteenth word.

**10.** Add *ose* to the end of the next to last word.

**Now how does the sentence read?**

# On the Wild Side, Part I

**Check out these amazing animal facts and then sort the animals according to the categories on page 46.**

The average **black bear** weighs 300 pounds; a polar bear weighs 1,800 pounds.

A **tiger** is so strong that it can drag an animal three times its own weight.

The word **koala** means "no water." Koalas get most of the water they need from the leaves they eat.

There are 40,000 muscles and tendons in an **elephant's** trunk alone.

A **chimpanzee** can lift six times its own weight.

Savi's **Pigmy Shrew** is only two-and-a-half-inches long. It weighs less than an ounce.

The **cheetah** is the fastest land mammal. It can run at a speed of 70 miles per hour.

**Yaks** can live at 20,000 feet above sea level.

A **kangaroo** can leap more than 40 feet in a single jump.

In one night, a **bat** can catch and eat several hundred mosquitoes.

The largest mammal is the **blue whale**. Females can be more than 100 feet long and weigh as much as 200 tons.

An adult **lion** weighs 600 pounds—that's 470 pounds more than a cheetah.

 **Try This!**  **Add More**  Think of one more thing for each group.

# On the Wild Side, Part II

**Classify the animals in the following categories:**

**Strongest**

_____
_____
_____
_____

**Fastest**

_____
_____
_____
_____

**Most Efficient**

_____
_____
_____
_____
_____

**Largest**

_____
_____
_____
_____
_____

**Smallest**

_____
_____
_____
_____
_____

**Create new categories that you can use to classify these animals.**

_____
_____
_____
_____
_____

**Try This!** **Organize Data** Flying foxes can live up to 17 years in captivity. Make a bar graph to compare the life spans of the following animals.

| Animal | Years | Animal | Years |
|--------|-------|--------|-------|
| llama | 20 | chicken | 9 |
| dog | 15 | armadillo | 6 |
| raccoon | 12 | toad | 25 |

# Get Set

• • • • • • • • • • •

**A set is a collection of people, objects, or numbers. The members of the set are alike in one or more ways. Here's an example:**

**5**

**3**  | 2  30  42  78  100 |  **17**

**101**          **49**

How are all the numbers *outside* the box the same? They are all *odd* numbers. How are all the numbers *inside* the box the same? They are all *even* numbers.

• • • • • • • • • • • • • • • • • • • • • • • • • • • • • • • • • • • • • • • • • • • • •

1.  Put the following letters into two sets. Put one set inside the box and the other set outside the box. Be ready to explain how you made your choices.

    A    B    Z    E    D
    I    G    O    C    U

2.  Arrange the following items into two sets. Put one set inside the circle and the other set outside the circle. Be ready to explain how you made your choices.

    jet      robin          glider
    kite     helicopter     sparrow
    eagle    hummingbird

3.

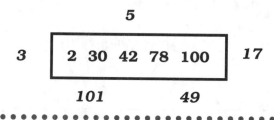

peas
lettuce       limes                lemons
beans         green grapes         grapefruit
broccoli      squash               bananas

**SET 1**                          **SET 2**

Set #1 is a set of _____. They are the color _____.

Set #2 is a set of _____. They are the color _____.

The place where Set #1 and Set #2 meet is a set of _____ and

_____. They are the colors _____ and _____.

**Try This!** **More Sets** Make a Venn diagram showing things that are red and things that you eat. The intersection should show red things that you eat.

47

# In Groups

· · · · · · · · · · · · ·

**Each of these lists has one item that does not belong. Find and cross out that item. Then explain why that item is out of place. The first one has been done for you.**

**1.**  zebra, lion, elephant, kitten  _The kitten is not a wild animal._

**2.**  tack, pliers, wrench, screwdriver  _____

**3.**  soccer, tennis, track, bowling  _____

**4.**  plum, melon, peach, apricot  _____

**5.**  New Mexico, Albany, Utah, Vermont  _____

**6.**  silver, ruby, brass, iron  _____

**7.**  pen, pencil, crayon, ruler  _____

**8.**  drums, oboe, saxophone, flute  _____

**9.**  leave, arrive, depart, go  _____

**10.**  horse, puppy, chick, duckling  _____

**11.**  newspaper, radio, book, magazine  _____

**12.**  eyes, nose, mouth, foot  _____

 **Try This!**  **Summarize** Write a title to name each group.

# Prime Time Numbers

**You can put numbers into groups because of ways they are the same and different. Early mathematicians discovered that most numbers can be written as the product of two numbers. Here are some examples:**

$4 \times 2 = 8$ $6 \times 6 = 36$

But some numbers cannot be written this way. They can only be shown as the product of 1 and the number itself. Here are some examples:

$1 \times 5 = 5$ $1 \times 17 = 17$

These are called *prime numbers.* A prime number is any number greater than 1 that can only be divided by itself and 1 evenly. Here are the first five prime numbers:

2, 3, 5, 7, 11

Circle all the prime numbers below:

| 1  | 2  | 3  | 4  | 5  | 6  | 7  | 8  | 9  | 10  |
|----|----|----|----|----|----|----|----|----|-----|
| 11 | 12 | 13 | 14 | 15 | 16 | 17 | 18 | 19 | 20  |
| 21 | 22 | 23 | 24 | 25 | 26 | 27 | 28 | 29 | 30  |
| 31 | 32 | 33 | 34 | 35 | 36 | 37 | 38 | 39 | 40  |
| 41 | 42 | 43 | 44 | 45 | 46 | 47 | 48 | 49 | 50  |
| 51 | 52 | 53 | 54 | 55 | 56 | 57 | 58 | 59 | 60  |
| 61 | 62 | 63 | 64 | 65 | 66 | 67 | 68 | 69 | 70  |
| 71 | 72 | 73 | 74 | 75 | 76 | 77 | 78 | 79 | 80  |
| 81 | 82 | 83 | 84 | 85 | 86 | 87 | 88 | 89 | 90  |
| 91 | 92 | 93 | 94 | 95 | 96 | 97 | 98 | 99 | 100 |

**Try This!** **More Primes** *Prime pairs* are two prime numbers that differ by two. For example: 3,5 or 5,7. Write some more prime pairs.

# Sequencing and Predicting Activities

Two important steps in the critical-thinking process are the ability to sequence details and to predict information based on prior knowledge and context clues. The activities in this section provide opportunities to help students learn and develop these skills.

Studies have shown that students who work in pairs or small groups tend to come up with more divergent responses. Therefore, you may wish to try a collaborative approach to some of these activities. These activities are especially well-suited to collaborative learning:
- Happy Birthday!
- The Survival Game
- Nim

Use this chart to help you identify activities to use with various curriculum areas. Instructions for teacher-led activities are on the activity pages, while notes for using the reproducibles follow the chart.

## Cross-Curricular Links

| Activity | Page | Content Area |
|---|---|---|
| Happy Birthday! | 52 | mathematics |
| The Survival Game | 53 | science/social studies |
| Pressed for Time | 54 | mathematics |
| Gomuku | 55 | math/multicultural |
| Nim | 56 | math/multicultural |
| Nile Numbers | 57 | math/multicultural/social studies |
| Order, Please | 58 | language arts |
| Palindrome Challenge | 59 | language arts |
| Big Questions | 60 | science/language arts |
| Build a Pyramid | 61–62 | language art/math |
| Secret of the Pyramids | 63 | social studies/math |

## Teacher Notes for Student Reproducibles
### Page 52: Happy Birthday!
Caution students to follow the directions carefully. If they come up with the wrong birthday, have them review their work to determine where the mistake is.

## Page 53: The Survival Game

Have students discuss the way they ranked the items. Explain that they should be prepared to defend their rankings. After students compare the way they ranked the items, have them work in groups to create graphs to show the results. For example, students might make bar graphs to show the five items ranked highest by the most class members.

## Page 54: Pressed for Time

Planning and scheduling time are important real-world skills. Discuss with the class how they might use such skills in their day-to-day lives.

## Page 55: Gomuku

Assign students to work with a partner to play this game. After students have played, discuss how Gomuku is similar to and different from tic-tac-toe.

## Page 56: Nim

In this strategy game, students must figure out how to leave an opponent with only one empty space. Encourage students to explain the strategies they use.

## Page 57: Nile Numbers

Students might enjoy researching the number systems of other ancient civilizations such as the Maya.

## Page 58: Order, Please

When students complete the page, have them share with the class how and why they ordered the items. How many different ways of ordering did the class use?

## Page 59: Palindrome Challenge

This activity may be difficult for some students. If it proves frustrating, pair these students with more verbal learners. Be sure to have students share their palindromes with the class.

## Page 60: Big Questions

This activity calls for students to think in global terms to make predictions. As a follow-up, have students choose one prediction and use it as the basis for a short story.

## Page 61-62: Build a Pyramid

In this activity, students must follow directions to make a paper pyramid. Display the finished pyramids with other Egyptian-related activities such as those on pages 57 and 63.

## Page 63: Secret of the Pyramids

Ask students to use each of the words in their pyramids in a complete sentence to show the word's meaning.

# Happy Birthday!

**Here's a different way to find out someone's birthday.**

Have a friend follow these instructions:

**1.** Write the number that stands for the month you were born. (January is 1, February is 2, March is 3, and so on)

**2.** Double the number.

**3.** Add 6.

**4.** Multiply the new number by 50.

**5.** Add the day you were born.

**6.** Subtract 365.

**7.** Add 65.

**8.** Make a slash between the second and third digit from the right. The numbers to the left of the slash stand for the month your friend was born; the numbers to the right stand for the day your friend was born.

 **Try This!** **An Age-Old Trick** Here's how to find out someone's age. Have a friend write his or her age on a piece of paper and keep it secret. Have your friend multiply the number by 3, add 12, divide by 3, and add 93. Have your friend tell you the number. Drop the first digit and add three to the remaining number to get your friend's age.

# The Survival Game

**Oh no! Your watch stopped and you missed the tour boat back to civilization. Looks like you'll be spending a while on an uninhabited tropical island. Below is a list of 30 items that might come in handy during your stay. Rank them in order of most important (1) to least important (30).**

_____ a bag of dried fruit
_____ 6 gallons of drinking water
_____ a jackknife
_____ a Walkman and tapes
_____ 10 bunches of bananas
_____ 10 cans of vegetables
_____ matches
_____ a copy of *Treasure Island*
_____ a blanket
_____ a bathing suit
_____ a deck of playing cards
_____ a hunting knife
_____ a can opener
_____ chewing gum
_____ a walkie-talkie
_____ soap
_____ ketchup and mustard
_____ a change of clothes
_____ a Frisbee
_____ a sack of potatoes
_____ a book called *Edible Tropical Plants*
_____ a flashlight
_____ a camera
_____ rope
_____ a compass
_____ 10 pounds of hamburger
_____ a device that converts salt water to drinking water
_____ a raincoat
_____ a comb
_____ a radio

 **Try This!**

**Compare with the Class** Discuss your rankings with classmates. How are they alike? How do they differ?

53

# Pressed for Time

So much to do and so little time! Here you are at the Old-Time Fair. You want to do everything, but that takes careful planning. Plan your schedule at the bottom of the page so you can fit in each event. The clocks show the different starting times of the events.

| | | |
|---|---|---|
| **Brass Band**<br>30 minute show | **11:15 AM** | **12:00 PM** |
| **Corn Shucking Contest**<br>45 minutes | **10:30 AM** | **1:00 PM** |
| **Sack Race**<br>30 minutes | **10:00 AM** | **12:00 PM** |
| **Pie-Eating Contest**<br>45 minute show | **10:00 AM** | **11:30 PM** |

| Schedule | Event | Time |
|---|---|---|
| | _____ | _____ |
| | _____ | _____ |
| | _____ | _____ |
| | _____ | _____ |

 **Try This!** **Make a Schedule** Plan how you will spend the hours between school and bedtime today.

54

# Gomuku

**People around the world like to play games! In America, many people play tic-tac-toe. In England, a similar game is called Noughts and Crosses. In Japan, it's called Gomuku.**

What do all these games have in common? In each one, the players have to figure out how to put X's and 0's in a certain order to win. Players also have to predict what their opponent will do.

Play a game of Gomuku with a friend. Here's how:

**1.** One player writes X's. The other player writes O's.

**2.** Partners take turns writing their mark anywhere on the game board. Players can write only one mark at a time.

**3.** The first player to get five marks in a row is the winner. The marks can be horizontal, vertical, or diagonal.

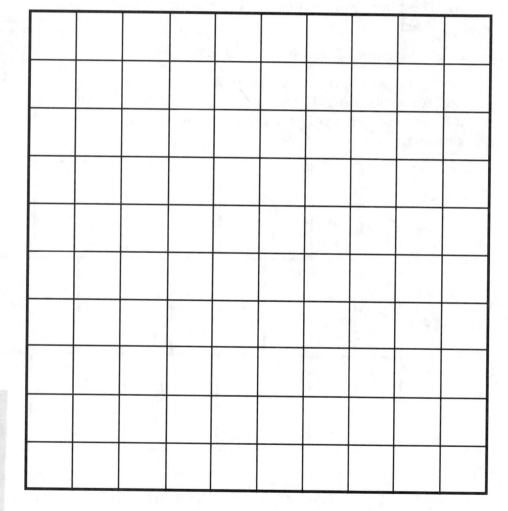

**Try This!**

**Play Again!** Teach Gomuku to someone at home.

# Nim
• • • • •

**Nim is a very old game played by people in many countries. Play Nim with a friend. It's easy!**

The object of the game is to get your opponent to write an X in the last space. Here's how to play:

**1.** Take turns.

**2.** Each player can write either one, two, or three X's in any one row on a single turn.

**3.** Take turns until only one empty space is left.

**4.** The player who writes an X in the last space loses.

A sample game of Nim might look like this:

Use the board to play the game. Make copies of the board so you can play more than once. After you play a few times, see if you can figure out a strategy for winning.

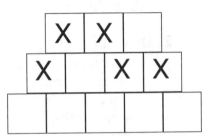

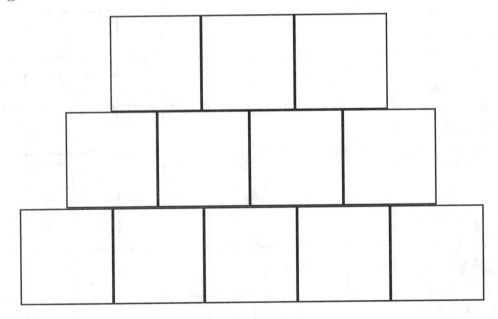

**Try This!** **New Nims** You can also play Nim with a different board. Try it with 2 boxes, 3 boxes, and 4 boxes; or try 5 boxes, 6 boxes, and 7 boxes. Does your strategy also work with these game boards?

# Nile Numbers
· · · · · · · · · · · · · · · · ·

**The Egyptians developed a system of writing, called hieroglyphics, that used picture symbols to represent numbers and objects. Here are the hieroglyphs for the numbers 1–1,000:**

| number | hieroglyph | object |
|--------|-----------|--------|
| 1 | \| | staff |
| 5 | \|\|\|\|\| | |
| 10 | ∩ | arch |
| 50 | ∩∩∩∩∩ | |
| 100 | ℓ | coiled rope |
| 1,000 | ⸙ | flower |

As you can see, there was no symbol for zero.

Time to translate! First, answer the following questions in our number system. Then, write the Egyptian numbers for these things.

| Question | Our Numbers | Egyptian Numbers |
|----------|-------------|------------------|
| **1.** Your age | _____ | _____ |
| **2.** Days in a week | _____ | _____ |
| **3.** Days in this month | _____ | _____ |
| **4.** Days in a year | _____ | _____ |
| **5.** Your house number | _____ | _____ |
| **6.** Students in your class | _____ | _____ |

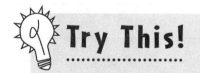 **Try This!**
· · · · · · · · · · · · · ·

**Today's Date** Write today's date (month/day/year) in hieroglyphics.

# Order, Please
• • • • • • • • • • • • • • • • • • •

**Below are lists of four items. You can order the items in the lists in different ways. Arrange each list in a way that makes sense to you. Write your explanation on the line provided.**

**For example: birdhouse, house, pup tent, castle**

You might arrange the items in order of size—from smallest to biggest: birdhouse, pup tent, house, castle; or you might choose to arrange them in alphabetical order: birdhouse, castle, house, pup tent. The choice is yours!

**1.** hour, second, day, minute _____

_____

**2.** Elizabeth Atkinson, Carlos Diaz, Andrea Martin, Bob Kin _____

_____

**3.** dawn, dusk, midnight, high noon _____

_____

**4.** seed, bud, flower, fruit _____

_____

**5.** neck, head, feet, knees _____

_____

**6.** California, Pennsylvania, Alaska, Hawaii _____

_____

**7.** peach, pea, cabbage, watermelon _____

_____

**Try This!** **Order More** Write down five foods. Order them in three different ways.

# Palindrome Challenge

**A palindrome is a word, phrase, or sentence that reads the same backwards as it does forwards. Probably the most famous examples are *Madam, I'm Adam* and Napoleon's *Able was I ere I saw Elba*. *Rise to vote, sir* and *A war at Tarawa* are also palindromes.**

Create your own original palindrome of at least three words. Be sure it makes sense!

**My palindrome:**

_____

_____

_____

_____

_____

_____

_____

**Try This!** **Illustrate It** Use the box above to draw a picture to go with your palindrome.

# Big Questions
· · · · · · · · · · · · · · · · · · ·

**Answer the following questions. There is no "right" answer.**

**1.** How would life be different if the sun never set?

_____

_____

**2.** How would life be different if people could only get from place to place by

walking?

_____

**3.** How would life be different if you were a bug instead of a human?

_____

**4.** How would life be different if there was no gravity?

_____

**5.** How would life be different if the sky was green?

_____

**6.** How would life be different if the United States, Europe, Africa, China,

etc., were all connected and there was only one land mass?

_____

_____

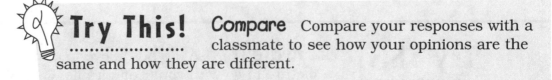 **Try This!** **Compare** Compare your responses with a
classmate to see how your opinions are the
same and how they are different.

# Build a Pyramid

**Built for Pharaoh Khufu, the Great Pyramid at Gaza was originally 480 feet high. Its base was 13 acres wide. When it was finished, the pyramid had more than two million blocks of limestone.**

Follow these directions to make a model of the Great Pyramid. (The real pyramid is 2,000 times larger than your model!) Here's what you'll need to make your model:

- scissors
- a ruler
- construction paper
- tape
- blue, red, and green crayons, pencils, or pens

Here's what to do:

**1.** Cut a piece of construction paper $8\frac{1}{2}$ " x  $8\frac{1}{2}$ ".

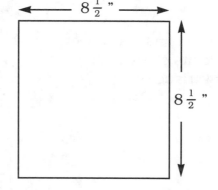

**2.** Use the blue crayon and your ruler to mark the midpoint on each side Draw a line to connect all four points.

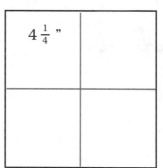

**3.** Measure 3 1/2" out from the intersection along each of the four lines. Mark those points with a dot.

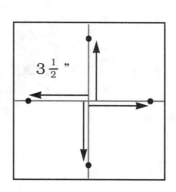

61

# Build a Pyramid cont.

**4.** Draw a red line from each corner of the paper to each point you marked. Cut along these lines and discard the scraps.

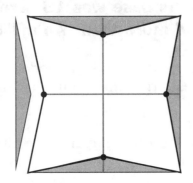

**5.** Draw a green line to connect the midpoints of each side forming 4 triangles.

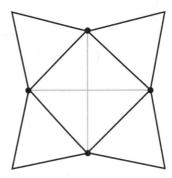

**6.** Fold along the lines and tape the edges to form your own great pyramid.

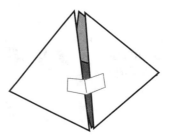

 **Try This!** **Think About It** Do you think a real Egyptian pyramid could be built today? Why or why not?

# Secret of the Pyramids

**Egypt's pyramids are the oldest stone buildings in the world. They were built nearly 5,000 years ago! You can make another kind of pyramid—with words. Play this game to find out how.**

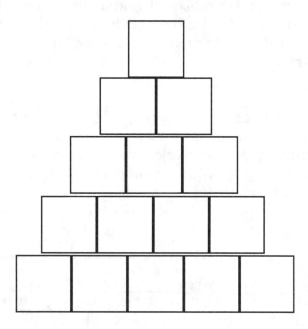

Here's how to play:

**1.** Write a single letter on the top row.

**2.** On the next row, write the same first letter and a new second letter to make a two-letter word.

**3.** On the third row, write the same first letter and two new letters to make a three-letter word.

**4.** Continue in the same way for rows four and five, always using the same first letter. Here's a sample:

 **Try This!** **Bigger Buildings** Add more levels to your pyramid to make longer and longer words.

# Activities for Inferring and Drawing Conclusions

From the time they are born, children make inferences about the world around them. Through body language, sounds, and visual clues, they are able to gather information and reflect on experience. The activities in this section will help strengthen students' critical-thinking skills by developing their ability to use multisensory clues and intelligences in making inferences and drawing conclusions.

You can present each activity as an independent lesson or integrate the activities into different curriculum areas as shown on the chart. You'll find that the activities increase in difficulty as you work through the section. Instructions for teacher-directed activities appear on the same page as the activity. Use the teacher notes that follow the chart for the student reproducibles.

## Cross-Curricular Links

| Activity | Page | Content Area |
|----------|------|--------------|
| That's Funny! | 66 | art/language arts |
| Surf and Turf | 67–69 | science/social studies |
| Constant Confusion | 70 | math/language arts |
| Shhh! | 71 | language arts |
| Q & A | 72 | language arts |
| Make a Wish | 73 | mathematics |

## Teacher Notes for Student Reproducibles

### Pages 67–69: Surf and Turf
You'll need to make double-sided copies of pages 68 and 69. You might make additional sets of this game to place in a science or social studies center. Encourage students to make up some cards of their own to add to the game.

### Page 70: Constant Confusion
Point out that *quintuplet* means five children born at the same time. Ask students what the word for four children born at the same time is. For six? seven?

### Page 71: Shhh!

This activity helps students practice spelling skills. Encourage them to use each word they decode in a written sentence.

### Page 72: Q & A

Point out that many of the logical answers are based on students' prior knowledge as well as the information given. Make students aware that their answers reflect the conclusions that they drew.

### Page 73: Make a Wish

Ask students to describe the strategies they use to solve this problem.
You may wish to have some students check the solution using real coins.

# That's Funny!

Have students bring in favorite comic strips from the newspaper. Make sure they clip comics with at least four panels. Have students cut off the last panel and pass their comics to another student. (Make sure that no student receives the comic he or she brought in.) Then invite students to complete the strips by drawing the last panel and filling in appropriate dialogue. Display the humorous results and ask students to describe how they came to their conclusions.

Variation: White-out the dialogue of several single-panel comics and distribute a copy to each student. Invite students to fill in appropriate dialogue. Share these with the class. Discuss the visual clues that students relied on to create their dialogue.

# Surf and Turf

**What's life like under the sea? How do creatures live in the forests? Learn more about the earth's oceans and forests by playing this game with a friend. Here's how:**

**1.** Cut out the double-sided playing cards on pages 68 and 69. You'll also need two copies of the game board below, one for each player.

**2.** Put all the cards in a stack, face up.

**3.** The first player picks the top card.

**4.** The player explains what's on the card and where it belongs. For example: Fish are sea creatures that belong in the ocean.

**5.** Players check the back of the card, and if the answer is right, the first player puts the card in the correct spot on his or her game board. If the first player is wrong, the card goes back in the stack.

**6.** Play ends when all the cards are in piles on the players' boards. The player with the most cards wins.

| | | |
|---|---|---|
| **sea plant** | **forest plant** | **forest creature** |
| **sea creature** | **products from the ocean** | **products from the forest** |

 **Try This!**    **More Cards** Make up a new card to add to the game.

| kelp | sea grass | sea kale | seaweed |
|---|---|---|---|
| elm trees | beech trees | pine trees | ferns |
| daisy | vines | Queen Anne's lace | orchid |
| water power | food | oil | fertilizers |
| fresh water | minerals such as sulfer, nickel and salt | fish | sponges |
| anemones | coral | crustaceans (crabs, lobsters) | dolphins |
| porpoises | plankton | wolves | bears |
| squirrels | caterpillars | fruit such as apples | tree pulp for paper |
| fuel | nuts and spices | wood for furniture | some medicines like quinine |

| | | | |
|---|---|---|---|
| sea<br>plant | sea<br>plant | sea<br>plant | sea<br>plant |
| forest<br>plant | forest<br>plant | forest<br>plant | forest<br>plant |
| forest<br>plant | forest<br>plant | forest<br>plant | forest<br>plant |
| products from<br>the ocean | products from<br>the ocean | products from<br>the ocean | products from<br>the ocean |
| sea<br>creature | sea<br>creature | products from<br>the ocean | products from<br>the ocean |
| sea<br>creature | sea<br>creature | sea<br>creature | sea<br>creature |
| forest<br>creature | forest<br>creature | sea<br>creature | sea<br>creature |
| products from<br>the forest | products from<br>the forest | forest<br>creature | forest<br>creature |
| products from<br>the forest | products from<br>the forest | products from<br>the forest | products from<br>the forest |

# Constant Confusion

**Mr. and Mrs. Dinkledorff have a problem. They have identical quintu-plets—Jessica, Jennifer, Justina, Judith, and Jackie—and they can't tell them apart. Read the clues below. Then give the Dinkledorffs a hand by writing each baby's name in the space provided.**

## CLUES

**A.** Judith is sitting between Jessica and Justina.

**B.** Jessica has no one on her right-hand side.

**C.** Jackie, the firstborn, always sits in front.

2. _____

1. _____

3. _____

4. _____

5. _____

 **Try This!**

**Draw Details** Help the Dinkledorffs so they don't get mixed up again. Draw details on each quintuplet so their parents can tell them apart.

# Shhh!
· · · · · · · ·

The club needs a new secret password, so Chris created a code. Your mission is to crack it! In each set of words below, the missing letter has been replaced by a shape. As you figure out what letter each shape stands for, fill it in at the bottom of the page to break the code.

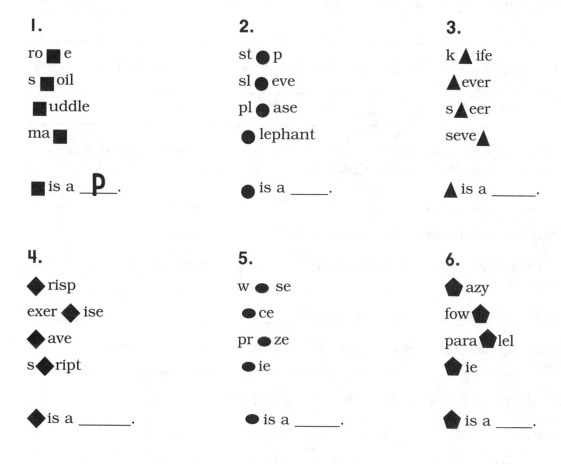

**1.**

ro ■ e

s ■ oil

■ uddle

ma ■

■ is a _P_ .

**2.**

st ● p

sl ● eve

pl ● ase

● lephant

● is a ____ .

**3.**

k ▲ ife

▲ ever

s ▲ eer

seve ▲

▲ is a ____ .

**4.**

◆ risp

exer ◆ ise

◆ ave

s ◆ ript

◆ is a _____ .

**5.**

w ● se

● ce

pr ● ze

● ie

● is a ____ .

**6.**

⬟ azy

fow ⬟

para ⬟ lel

⬟ ie

⬟ is a ____ .

The password is:

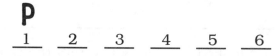

P
_1_  _2_  _3_  _4_  _5_  _6_

**Try This!**  **More Codes** Create your own secret code.
· · · · · · · · · · · · ·

# Q & A

● ● ● ● ● ● ● ● ● ●

**Some questions have only one answer. Other questions, however, have more than one answer. See how many answers you can come up with for these questions.**

1. "Be sure not to lose these," Sammi said as she and her friends left on a week's camping trip. What did Sammi hand her friends? _____

   _____

2. How would you know whether someone had lit a fire in the grill if you hadn't been there at the time? _____

   _____

3. Dad looked out the car window and said, "This would not be a good place to grow crops." How did he reach this conclusion? _____

   _____

4. How can you tell if a person is very strong? _____

5. "There must have been a wedding here," Frank said. How did he come to this conclusion? _____

6. How are a cow and a chicken the same? _____

7. If you saw a hole in the ground, how could you conclude if it was deep or shallow? _____

8. How could you tell it was windy, without going outside? _____

   _____

9. About 70 percent of the earth is covered with water. The remaining 30 percent is land. People don't live on all that land. Why not? _____

   _____

10. If you were in the woods and saw what looked like lights through the trees, what might they be? _____

   _____

 **Try This!** **Talk About It** Discuss and compare your answers with the class.

# Make a Wish

Every week, Jeffrey cleans out the wishing well at the park.  How much money did he find this week? Use these clues to figure out how many pennies, nickels, and dimes he found. Write your answer on the corresponding basket

## CLUES

1. He finds at least one penny, one nickel, and one dime.
2. He has a total of 14 coins.
3. The coins add up to 56 cents.
4. He has more nickels than dimes.
5. He has the same number of pennies as nickels.

 **Try This!** **Another Problem** Change the coins and rewrite the problem. See if a classmate can solve it.

# Evaluating Activities

**Before students begin the activities in this section, explain that evaluating means making a judgment about something. Point out that people often make evaluations in their everyday lives—judgments about other people, events, and things they see; food they eat; and books they read. Invite volunteers to share an evaluation they made today.**

The activities in this section will guide students through the process of evaluating. You can use each activity as a complete lesson or weave the activities into other curriculum studies. Within this section, the activities are arranged from easiest to most difficult. Instructions for teacher-led activities appear on the same page as the activity. Teacher notes for the student reproducibles follow the chart.

## Cross-Curricular Links

| Activity | Page | Content Area |
|---|---|---|
| You Decide | 76–80 | science |
| My Hero! | 81 | social studies |
| The Sports Hall of Fame | 82 | physical education |
| Fact or Opinion? | 83 | language arts/social studies |
| Space, the Final Frontier | 84 | science |
| Twins? | 85 | language arts |
| My Book Review | 86 | language arts |
| About Me | 87 | language arts |

## Teacher Notes for Student Reproducibles

### Pages 76–80: You Decide

In this activity, students organize information according to its importance. Stress that while ideas may differ, students should be able to defend their reasoning. Make copies of each page and have students create their double-sided cards by cutting along the dotted lines and folding the cards along the center line to create a front and a back. They can either paste the sides together or bind them with tape.

## Page 81: My Hero!

Before students complete this page, engage them in a discussion of why they admire some people. List the characteristics and qualities mentioned on the chalkboard. Make the point that a person doesn't have to be rich or famous to be admired. In fact, many rich and famous people aren't particularly admirable at all. After students complete the page, invite them to share their lists with the class.

## Page 82: The Sports Hall of Fame

Ask students if they think that sports figures have an obligation to be good role models as well as outstanding athletes. Then discuss which sports figures students feel are good role models.

## Page 83: Fact or Opinion?

Follow up this activity by asking students to analyze a news article to determine which statements are facts and which are opinions. Explain beforehand that a news article should contain facts which can be substantiated, whereas an editorial includes the opinion of the editors.

## Page 84: Space, the Final Frontier

Invite students to share their completed planning forms. Discuss the skills and qualities students identified for their crew members. Encourage students to explain their thinking.

## Page 85: Twins?

After students complete this activity, discuss how they might use these comparisons in metaphors and similes. Give an example such as *A sweater is a blanket for the body.* Challenge the class to see how many interesting figures of speech they can create.

## Page 86: My Book Review

Compile students' book reviews into a class folder and place it in a reading center. Encourage students to use it as a reference when selecting reading material.

## Page 87: About Me

This page provides an opportunity for students to think about themselves in a positive way. If some students say they can't think of answers for some items, assign partners who can offer constructive observations.

# You Decide
∙ ∙ ∙ ∙ ∙ ∙ ∙ ∙ ∙ ∙ ∙ ∙ ∙

**Many great scientists and inventors have helped the world. For example, Dr. Christiaan Barnard performed the first human heart transplant and Louis Pasteur discovered how to kill germs in milk. These are important discoveries, but which ones were the most important? You decide!**

First, cut out the "Scientist Cards." Then, read the information on both sides. Decide which inventions were the most important and why. To show your choices, arrange the cards from most to least important. Once you have made your choices, discuss them with the class.

front                                       back

**The *Eagle***

**Neil Armstrong**

*person*: Neil Armstrong

*born*: 1930

*birthplace*: Ohio

*accomplishment*: First person to set foot on the moon

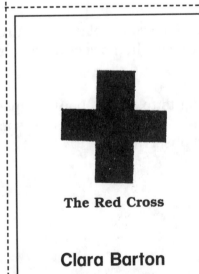

**The Red Cross**

**Clara Barton**

*person*: Clara Barton

*dates*: 1821-1912

*birthplace*: Massachu-setts

*accomplishment*: Founded the American Red Cross

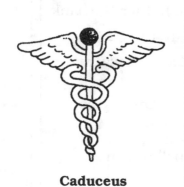

**Caduceus**

**Elizabeth Blackwell**

*person*: Elizabeth Blackwell

*dates*: 1821–1910

*birthplace:* England

*accomplishment:* First female doctor; fought for equal rights for women in the medical profession

**Rachel Carson**

*person*: Rachel Carson

*dates*: 1907-1964

*birthplace:* Pennsylvania

*accomplishment:* Ecologist who revealed the dangers of DDT

**George Washington Carver**

*person*: George Washington Carver

*dates*: 1864-1943

*birthplace:* Missouri

*accomplishment:* Research on peanuts and sweet potatoes; among the first great African-American scientists

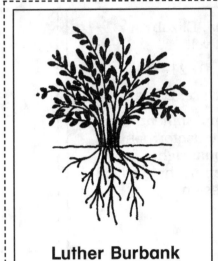

**Luther Burbank**

*person*: Luther Burbank

*dates*: 1849-1926

*birthplace:* Massachu-
setts

*accomplishment:* Dis-
covered many
plant variations;
cross-pollination

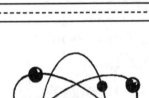

**Atomic Symbol**

**Marie Curie**

*person:* Marie Curie

*dates* :1867–1934

*birthplace*: Poland
*accomplishment:* Dis-
covered radium
and polonium

**Charles Darwin**

*person*: Charles Darwin

*dates*: 1809–1882

*birthplace:* England

*accomplishment:* For-
mulated the theory of
natural selection

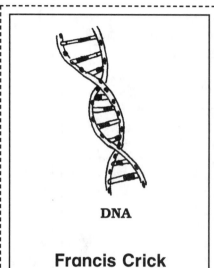

**DNA**

**Francis Crick**

*person*: Francis Crick

*born*: 1916

*birthplace:* England

*accomplishment*:
co-discoverer of DNA

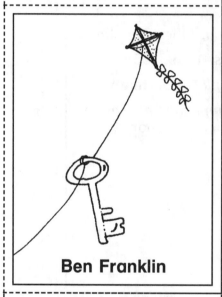

**Ben Franklin**

*person*: Ben Franklin

*dates*: 1706–1790

*birthplace:* Massachu-
setts

*accomplishment*:
experiments with
electricity, lenses
(invented bifocal
glasses)

**Charles Goodyear**

*person*: Charles
Goodyear

*dates*: 1800–1860

*birthplace:* Connecticut

*accomplishment*: Invent-
ed process
to create rubber
("vulcanization")

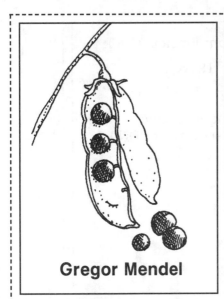

**Gregor Mendel**

*person*: Gregor Mendel

*dates*: 1822–1884

*birthplace:* Czech

*accomplishment:* Formulated gene theory

**Albert Einstein**

*person*: Albert Einstein

*dates*: 1849–1955

*birthplace:* Germany

*accomplishment:* Theory of nuclear fission

# My Hero!
· · · · · · · · · · · · ·

**List the five people you admire most. These people can be from the past or the present.**

Hero 1. _____

Hero 2. _____

Hero 3. _____

Hero 4. _____

Hero 5. _____

**Think of a trait that all the people you admire have in common. Write it below.**

_____

**Now, think of a special quality that makes each of the people unique. Write a different trait for each of them below.**

Hero 1. _____

Hero 2. _____

Hero 3. _____

Hero 4. _____

Hero 5. _____

 **Try This!**
· · · · · · · · · · · · · · ·

**Define It** Write a definition of what a hero or heroine is.

# The Sports Hall of Fame

**Imagine that you have been asked to nominate a person for the Sports Hall of Fame. Who would you nominate and why? Your choice can be a professional athlete from the past or present, a friend, a parent, a coach, or a teacher.**

Complete the form below.

## SPORTS HALL OF FAME NOMINATION FORM

**A.** Name of person nominated: _____

**B.** Main sport that he or she plays: _____

**C.** Number of years playing the sport: _____

**D.** Three reasons why the person should be inducted into the Sports Hall of Fame:

    **1.** _____

       _____

    **2.** _____

       _____

    **3.** _____

       _____

**Try This!** **Gather Evidence** Find newspaper or magazine articles that support your choice for the Sports Hall of Fame or write some of your own.

# Fact or Opinion?

**A fact is something that you can prove. Facts are true. This statement is an example of a fact: Halloween is an October holiday. An opinion is a personal belief that may or may not be true. Many people may share an opinion, but that does not make it a fact. This statement is an example of an opinion: Halloween is the best holiday. In the blanks below, write an F if the statement is a fact and an O if it is an opinion. When you're done, discuss your answers with the class.**

_____ 1. *Island of the Blue Dolphins* is a great book.

_____ 2. By the time a child is five years old, he or she knows about 5,000 words.

_____ 3. Charles Schultz's best character is Charlie Brown.

_____ 4. Rainbows are created when drops of water are hit by light and form prisms.

_____ 5. Mercury, Venus, Earth, Mars, Jupiter, Saturn, Uranus, Neptune, and Pluto are planets.

_____ 6. Sixth grade is more fun than fifth grade.

_____ 7. The first home television set, built in 1928, had a screen that measured 3 inches by 4 inches.

_____ 8. George Washington's face appears on quarters.

_____ 9. The Empire State Building can sway up to two inches in high winds.

_____ 10. Americans eat more than two billion pounds of pasta per year.

_____ 11. Cats make nice pets.

_____ 12. No two people have the same fingerprints.

_____ 13. Sign language is the language used third most often in America, after English and Spanish.

_____ 14. You should use mustard on hot dogs and ketchup on hamburgers.

_____ 15. Red and blue are primary colors.

_____ 16. Pretzels taste great when you eat them one at a time.

_____ 17. The New York Mets won the World Series in 1969.

_____ 18. My nose is too long.

_____ 19. Jupiter is the largest planet in our solar system.

_____ 20. Alligators and crocodiles are both endangered animals.

 **Try This!** **Check It Out** Find a reference to support each statement that you marked as a fact.

# Space, the Final Frontier

**Imagine that NASA has just picked you to command the first space colony! The colony will be near the Omega galaxy frontier. You know this is a tough job, full of danger. But you're ready for the challenge.**

**Before you leave, you have to do some planning. Complete the form to set up your crew.**

**Omega Galaxy Mission**

Commander: _____

Star Date: _____ Rank: _____

As the commander, you must select a crew. List some skills the crew will need. Explain why each skill is so important.

| Skill | Reason |
|-------|--------|
| _____ | _____ |
| _____ | _____ |
| _____ | _____ |
| _____ | _____ |
| _____ | _____ |
| _____ | _____ |

Now, list four people to serve with you on this important mission. Explain why you chose each person.

| Person | Reason |
|--------|--------|
| _____ | _____ |
| _____ | _____ |
| _____ | _____ |
| _____ | _____ |

 **Try This!** **Want Ad** Use the information on your form to write a want ad for a crew member.

# Twins?
• • • • • • • • •

Some things look alike and act alike. Other things don't look that much alike—but are still very much alike. Tell how each pair of objects below are alike. List as many ways as you can.

**Objects**                    **How Alike**

1. sweater/blanket            _____

                              _____

2. wind/water                 _____

                              _____

3. fish/soap                  _____

                              _____

4. puppy/baby                 _____

                              _____

5. pencil/candle              _____

                              _____

6. oatmeal/bread              _____

                              _____

7. rain/tears                 _____

                              _____

8. lion/eagle                 _____

                              _____

9. comb/saw                   _____

                              _____

10. spring/youth              _____

                              _____

**Try This!**
• • • • • • • • • • • • • • • • • •

**Write a Poem** Use one of your comparisons in a poem.

85

# My Book Review

**One of the best ways to find out about good books is from other readers. You can tell friends about the books you read, too. First, pick a book and read it carefully. Then answer the questions below. When you're done, share your book review with the class.**

Title: _____

Author: _____

Illustrator (if any): _____

Plot summary (Don't give away the ending!): _____

_____

What I liked about the book: _____

_____

What I didn't like about the book: _____

_____

Another story this book reminds me of and why: _____

_____


I'd give this book _____ stars

Star Rating System

★ = Blah          ★ ★ = OK          ★ ★ ★ = Pretty Good

★ ★ ★ ★ = Very Good          ★ ★ ★ ★ ★ = Totally Awesome!

 **Try This!**  **Illustrate It** Draw a character or scene from the book to go with your review.

Name _____

# About Me
· · · · · · · · · · · · ·

You evaluate books, places, and things
every day.  Now, take a look at yourself by
answering each of the following questions:

1. I am especially good at _____

2. I am a good friend because I _____

3. People can trust me because I _____

4. One of the best things about me is _____

5. I am fun to be with when I _____

6. I help my family by _____

7. I help my friends by _____

8. I help my community by _____

9. I try to make the world a better place by _____

10. I like myself because I _____

 **Try This!**
· · · · · · · · · · · · · · ·

**More Ideas** Think of a goal that you have for
yourself. Write a plan for how you will reach it.

# Analyzing Activities

Ask students if they have ever been faced with a very tricky problem—something they could not solve easily. It might have been a problem in math, difficulty finding a lost item, or a problem deciding how to make the best use of their time.

Point out that no matter what the problem, a good way to solve it is to analyze it. Explain that analyzing a problem means breaking it down into smaller parts or "steps" and then thinking about each step. Tell students that when they analyze a problem this way, they are better able to predict possible outcomes and propose solutions that make sense.

After you have discussed this process, you may wish to model it by working through some of the activities in this section. Consider using Puzzle Pattern, Dare Dare, and Flower Power as activities to model analysis skills.

After you have finished modeling the activity, ask students to comment on the way you arrived at your solution.

The chart shows related curriculum areas for each activity. Use the teacher notes that follow to introduce the student reproducibles.

## Cross-Curricular Links

| Activity | Page | Content Area |
| --- | --- | --- |
| A Million-and-One Uses | 90 | language arts/science |
| Puzzle Pattern | 91 | mathematics |
| Scavenger Hunt | 92 | language arts |
| What Does It Represent? | 93 | multicultural studies |
| Dare Dare | 94 | language arts |
| Flower Power | 95 | mathematics |
| Odd Couples | 96 | science/social studies |
| Divide and Conquer | 97 | mathematics |
| Riddle Me This | 98 | social studies/language arts |
| Amazing Analogies | 99 | language arts |
| Puzzling Problems | 100 | language arts/ mathematics/science |
| Multiple Uses | 101 | science/art |

## Teacher Notes for Student Reproducibles
### Page 91: Puzzle Pattern
Display the puzzle patterns that students create. Have students write a caption for their puzzles explaining how the pattern changes.

## Page 92: Scavenger Hunt

You might assign students to work with partners to complete this activity. Follow up by bringing the class together to share results. Which are the funniest answers? the most original? You might also have students create charts or graphs to show these results.

## Page 93: What Does It Represent?

Point out that we use symbols every day. Have students compile a list of some of the common symbols they know. Next to each, describe what it stands for.

## Page 94: Dare Dare

After students make up their own word puzzles, create a bulletin-board display. Challenge the class to solve all the puzzles.

## Page 95: Flower Power

Ask a volunteer to explain to the class, step-by-step, how to solve the problem. Encourage students who used other strategies to share them as well.

## Page 96: Odd Couples

This comparing activity helps students focus on similarities between two items. After students complete the page, challenge them to identify differences as well.

## Page 97: Divide and Conquer

Call on different volunteers to come to the chalkboard and show how they divided the shapes.

## Page 98: Riddle Me This

Point out that most riddles rely on a play of words in which a word has more than one meaning. Have students identify this aspect of the riddles on page 98.

## Page 99: Amazing Analogies

If students are not familiar with analogies, you will want to review some of the kinds of relationships that they show for example—part/whole, synonyms, antonyms, descriptive attributes, tools and users. For students who have difficulty with this assignment, you might assign them a partner to work with.

## Page 100: Puzzling Problems

You might have students work in small groups to complete this page. If students wish to try out their solutions, they will need to bring in the required materials beforehand. Set aside time for each group to present its solutions.

## Page 101: Multiple Uses

This activity calls for students to propose alternatives for a common object. After students complete the page and share their ideas, compile a list of all the alternatives. Ask the class to rank them according to originality, likelihood, and other criteria.

# A Million-and-One Uses

Here's an activity that encourages students to take a fresh look at some familiar objects. Write the names of these objects on slips of paper and put them in a hat:

a piece of paper
a sheet
a pillow
a book
a chair
a cup
a piece of string
a box
a rubber band

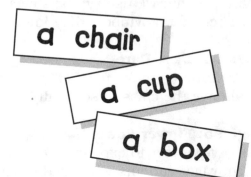

Divide the class into small groups. Have each group draw a slip from the hat. Then give the groups 15 minutes to brainstorm new uses for that object. For example, if the group selected "a piece of paper," its list might look something like this:

> fold into a fan to keep cool
> fold into a cup for drinking
> crumple into a ball to play catch
> use as a bookmark

After the brainstorming session, invite the groups to share their lists with the class.

# Puzzle Pattern
· · · · · · · · · · · · · · · · · · · ·

**The following designs have been created by moving a piece of the puzzle. Solve the puzzle by predicting how it must change to continue the pattern.**

**1.** Study squares 1 and 2.
How did 1 change to create 2?

**1.**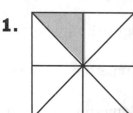

**2.**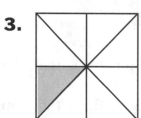

**2.** Look at square 3. How is it different from 2?
Predict how 4 will change.

**3.**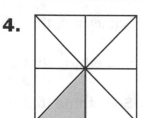

**4.**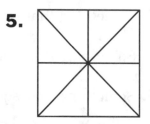

**3.** Look at 4 to see if you were correct.
Based on this pattern, what will 5 look like?
Fill in 5.

**5.**

 **Try This!**
· · · · · · · · · · · · · · · · ·

**More Patterns** Create your own changing pattern on the back of this paper. Then trade papers with a friend to see if he or she is able to predict how your pattern changed.

# Scavenger Hunt
· · · · · · · · · · · · · · · · · · · ·

**Guess what! You're going on a scavenger hunt, and you don't even have to leave your desk. Think of something that fits each of the descriptions below and write it in the blank.**

1. Something you toss: _____

2. Something that is messy: _____

3. Something that changes shape: _____

4. Something that you should not walk on: _____

5. Something that you shake: _____

6. Something that smells fantastic: _____

7. Something that you heat: _____

8. Something that changes color: _____

9. Something that you freeze: _____

10. Something that you stir: _____

11. Something that is loud: _____

12. Something that grows: _____

13. Something that opens: _____

14. Something that you carry: _____

15. Something that squeaks: _____

 **Try This!**
· · · · · · · · · · · · · ·

**Act It Out** Choose one or two of the things you wrote and act it out. Can the class guess your answer to the Scavenger Hunt clue?

# What Does It Represent?

**Throughout Asia, the crane is a symbol for good luck. Similarly, an olive branch symbolizes peace, and a white flag means surrender. Write a sentence to explain what each of the following symbols means to you.**

a dove _____

an eagle _____

the American flag _____

a red rose _____

a fox _____

an owl _____

a wedding ring _____

a four-leaf clover _____

 **Try This!**
...............

**More Symbols** What do these symbols mean: skull and crossbones, yellow traffic light, cornucopia?

# Dare Dare
• • • • • • • • • • • •

**What's dare dare? Well, there are two "dares," so it must be double dare! I "double dare" you to figure out these word puzzles:**

---

**10 AC**

You can analyze this one
by the way it sounds: 10 = Ten.
So 10 AC is Tennessee!

---

boy **Blue**

You can analyze this one
by the way it looks: a
little "boy" and a big
"blue" = Little Boy Blue!

---

**Analyze these four puzzles. Write your answers on the lines.**

**1.**

get
get      IT!
get
get

_____

**2.**

head
heels

_____

**3.**

s    o    t    m    a    c    h

_____

**4.**

wheel
wheel          drive
wheel
wheel

_____

**Try This!** ••••••••••••  Your Own Puzzles Make up some word puzzles of your own. See if your classmates can figure them out.

# Flower Power
· · · · · · · · · · · · · · · · · ·

**Matilda wants to plant flowers. She wants to have an equal number of tulips and daffodils in yellow, orange, and white. But when Matilda bought a bag of bulbs, she didn't know how many of each color she had. Use the facts below to see how many flowers of each color Matilda has.**

**1.** Of the three colors, each group has a different number of members.
**2.** Twice as many tulips are orange as daffodils are yellow.
**3.** Four times as many tulips are white as daffodils are orange.
**4.** An equal number of tulips are orange as daffodils are white.
**5.** Three more daffodils are yellow as tulips are yellow.
**6.** No tulips are yellow.

|           | Orange | Yellow | White | Total |
|-----------|--------|--------|-------|-------|
| Daffodils |        |        |       | 10    |
| Tulips    |        |        |       |       |
| Totals    |        |        |       | 20    |

**Try This!** **Illustrate It** Draw what the garden will look like. Color in the flowers.

# Odd Couples
· · · · · · · · · · · · · · · · · · · ·

**The following pairs may seem mismatched at first glance, but they actually have a lot in common. Think about these "odd couples." Then write down three things these partners have in common.**

**1. kitten/baby**

_____

_____

_____

**2. computer/typewriter**

_____

_____

_____

**3. magazine/radio**

_____

_____

_____

**4. worm/snail**

_____

_____

_____

**5. water/wind**

_____

_____

_____

**6. bubble/balloons**

_____

_____

_____

**7. spring/birth**

_____

_____

_____

**8. 3/7**

_____

_____

_____

**9. lion/elephant**

_____

_____

_____

**10. tomatoes/cherries**

_____

_____

_____

 **Try This!** **Share and Compare** Work with a partner to share and compare responses.

96

# Divide and Conquer

Below are a series of shapes. Analyze each shape to see how many different ways you can divide it into four equal pieces. The first square is done for you. (Note: You may not be able to divide a shape into four equal pieces at all.)

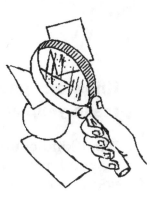

**1.**

**2.**

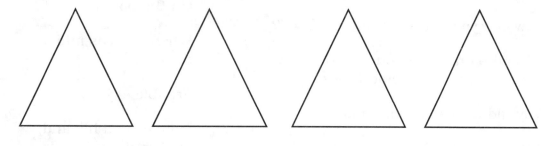

**3.**

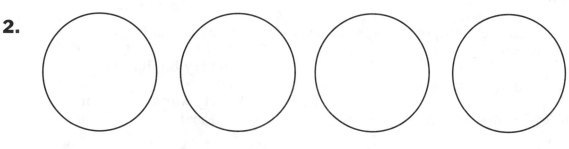

**4.**

**Try This!** .............. **Think Thirds** How many different ways can you divide each shape into thirds?

# Riddle Me This

**Know any good jokes, riddles, and puns? Here are some that will make you laugh:**

What kind of dress do you have that you never wear?

**Your address.**

What's the tallest building in your city?

**The library—it has the most stories.**

**Draw a line matching each joke to its answer.**

| Joke | Answer |
|------|--------|
| **1.** What's easy to get into but hard to get out of? | Because it's too far to walk |
| **2.** Why did the man pour veggies all over the world? | Nine |
| **3.** When is a car not a car? | Very big hands |
| **4.** If 2 is company and 3 is a crowd, what's 4 and 5? | He wanted peas on Earth. |
| **5.** How can you make a hamburger roll? | On the bottom |
| **6.** If I had 6 oranges in one hand and 8 in the other, what would I have? | When it turns into a driveway |
| **7.** Why did the candle fall in love? | Trouble |
| **8.** Where was the Declaration of Independence signed? | Take it up a hill and push it down. |
| **9.** Why do ducks fly south? | He met the perfect match. |

 **Try This!**

**Keep Laughing** Make some jokes of your own by writing a funny answer to these questions:

**What's worse than finding a worm in your apple?**

**What year do frogs like best?**

# Amazing Analogies

Analogies show relationships between pairs of words.

Analogies look like this:   **yolk : egg :: pit : cherry.**

You read this analogy by saying: **"Yolk is to egg as pit is to cherry."**
In this example, the relationship is part to whole: a yolk is part of an
egg, and a pit is part of a cherry.

**Complete the analogies below.  Then write the analogy statement.
The first one has been done for you.**

I. dry : desert :: wet : __ocean__   Dry is to desert as wet is to ocean.

2. palm : hand :: sole : _____

3. three : triangle :: four : _____

4. Venus : planet :: poodle : _____

5. pears : trees :: pumpkins: _____

6. turkey : Thanksgiving :: witch : _____

7. shades : windows :: rugs : _____

8. swimming : water :: sledding : _____

9. grapes : cluster :: bananas : _____

10. teacher : chalk :: artist : _____

11. book : read :: television : _____

12. sugar : sweet :: lemon : _____

 **Try This!**   **Name the Relationships** Reread the
analogies, then identify the kind of
relationship each one shows.

# Puzzling Problems

**When you analyze a problem, you break it into smaller parts to find the answer. You look for clues in the problem. You add these clues to what you already know. Some problems have only one answer, but other problems have many answers.**

**Analyze these problems to come up with solutions. Write your answers on the lines provided.**

**1.** How can you make an unshelled hard-boiled egg balance on its end?

_____

**2.** How can two people stand on the same sheet of newspaper, face to face, so they can't possibly touch each other? (Hint: Their hands aren't tied and you can't tear the sheet of newspaper.)

_____

**3.** A boy went to the dentist to get a cavity filled. The boy was the dentist's son, but the dentist was not the boy's father. How can this be?

_____

**4.** You have ten pennies arranged like this. Make the pennies face the other way. You can only move 3 pennies.

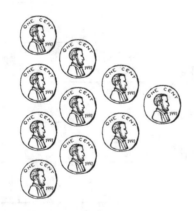

**5.** You have two bottles. One holds five quarts. One holds three quarts. You need exactly four quarts. How can you do it?

_____

 **Try This!** **Write About It** Write a step-by-step account of how you solved one of the problems on this page.

# Multiple Uses

Often, there is more than one way to use an object. For example, a brick is usually used as part of a building wall, but some people use bricks as doorstops, too.

Suppose you had a shoe box. Think about how you might use it for each of the following purposes. Write a description of your idea.

1. As a pet's home _____

_____

2. To study volume in math _____

_____

3. As a container for something special _____

_____

4. As part of a game _____

_____

5. In an art project _____

_____

 **Try This!** **Your Own Idea** Think of another way you might use a shoe box. On another sheet of paper, draw a picture or write a description.

# Synthesizing Activities

Explain that synthesizing means putting information together. Tell students that in these activities they will get a chance to use what they know to figure out new things. Encourage students to take their time and think carefully as they work.

Many of these activities are ideally suited to cooperative groups. If you decide to group students, make sure that everyone has a specific task to perform—one that is suited to the students' skills, strengths, and interests. Activities that lend themselves to this approach include:

• Build a Better Mousetrap
• Invention Convention
• Change the World

Use the chart to help you identify activities that tie in with other content areas.

## Cross-Curricular Links

| Activity | Page | Content Area |
|---|---|---|
| Response Rally | 104–105 | language arts |
| A Coat of Arms | 106 | social studies |
| Build a Better Mousetrap | 107 | science/industrial arts |
| Rainbow Creations | 108 | art/mathematics |
| Deer Me! | 109 | science |
| Magic Squares | 110 | mathematics/multicultural |
| All Mixed Up | 111 | science |
| A Yellow Submarine | 112 | science |
| Invention Convention | 113 | science |
| Change the World | 114 | social studies |

## Teacher Notes for Student Reproducibles

### Page 106: A Coat of Arms
Some students might be interested in learning about the symbolism of colors and incorporate this knowledge into their coat of arms. Set aside time for students to share their designs. Have students explain the pictures, colors, and words they used.

### Page 107: Build a Better Mousetrap
In this activity, students make alterations or improvements to a given object. Some students might want to build models from their drawings. Have students share their work with the class.

### Page 108: Rainbow Creations
Point out that the arch in a rainbow is part of nature, and people have used this same shape in buildings and other items since ancient times. Ask volunteers to create a bulletin-board display of arches that includes students' designs.

### Page 109: Deer Me!
This activity calls for students to propose alternative solutions to a real-life problem. After students complete the page, have them share their ideas. Then have the class decide which solutions would work best.

### Page 110: Magic Squares
You might have students work with partners to check one another's work. If students make up their own magic squares, compile them in a folder and place them in your math center.

### Page 111: All Mixed Up
Consider assigning this page for students to complete at home or plan to do the activity just before lunch. Then serve the class salad topped with students' dressing. See the answer key for an explanation of the experiment.

### Page 112: A Yellow Submarine
You may wish to have the class do this experiment together. See the answer key for an explanation of how submarines rise and sink.

### Page 114: Change the World!
Students may wish to do some research before completing this page. You might also compile a list of things that they themselves could actually do to help address some of these issues.

# Response Rally

Here's a fun way to help your students build synthesis skills. Pose the following questions one at a time, challenging students to write down as many possible answers for each question as they can. When you're done, discuss students' responses. Encourage students to explain their answers.

1. Imagine your mother said to you, "I am glad you had an egg with toast before you went to school this morning." She did not prepare your breakfast; she did not see you eat it. How did she know what you ate?

2. Plants native to one region are found all over the world. Why?

3. How are animals and plants similar? How are they different?

4. Which things do you wish had *never* been invented? Why?

5. Why are homes around the world different?

6. If you could invent anything in the world, what would it be and why?

7. Name some books in which animals speak like people.

8. If you could be any age at all, what age would you be and why?

9. Name as many hobbies as you can.

10. Imagine you had a time machine that could take you backward or forward in time. Where would you go and why?

11. If you were a superhero, who would you be and why?

12. List as many uses for paper as you can imagine.

13. What one thing would you do to improve the world?

14. Why do people speak different languages?

15. Imagine your parents said to you, "We wish you would not go out to play so early in the morning." They did not see you leave or enter the house; they did not see you outside. How did they know you went outside?

16. What would the United States be like if there was no government?

17. Who is your favorite writer? Why?

18. Do you wish dinosaurs were still alive? Why or why not?

19. Which sport do you think is the best? Why?

20. What would the world be like if people didn't have to sleep?

# A Coat of Arms

A family coat of arms is a shield with pictures that represent your family. For example, if your family lives in the mountains, loves baseball, and travels a lot, your coat of arms might include a mountain, a baseball diamond, and a car with suitcases on its roof. Think about what makes your family unique. Then design a family coat of arms below.

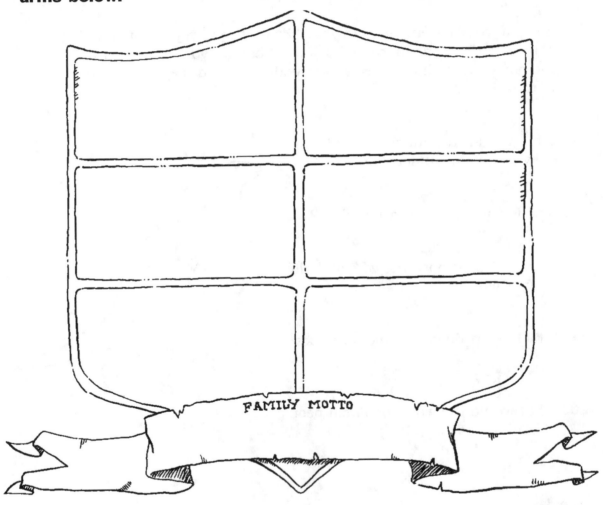

FAMILY MOTTO

**Fun Fact:** Knights in 12th-century Europe had individual patterns put on their battle shields and their coats. That is why a family crest is called a "coat of arms."

 **Try This!** Make a Motto A coat of arms usually includes a saying or a motto. Add a motto to your coat of arms.

# Build a Better Mousetrap

Even things that are well designed can be improved. For example, wouldn't it be nice if your lunch box had an alarm system to keep cookie snatchers away? Suppose your bike had wings so that you could fly over to a friend's house? Well here's your chance to make some changes for the better. Choose one of the items from list A and add as many practical and far-out features from list B—and your imagination—as you like. Draw a picture of your "super-object" in the box below.

| A | | B | |
|---|---|---|---|
| roller skates | eyeglasses | pockets | mirror |
| skateboard | bike | buzzer | parachute |
| book | bed | CD player | flashing lights |
| sneakers | lunch box | wings | motor |

**Try This!** Explain It Write a description of your new design. Explain how it works.

# Rainbow Creations

Think about a rainbow's special shape. Brainstorm a list of things that have a rainbow's arched shape, such as a doorway, a tunnel, a horseshoe, and a boomerang. Now, think of some other things that could have a rainbow's arched shape. Sketch your rainbow creations below. Be sure to include a description of each. When you're done, you may want to do final drawings of your creations on a separate sheet of paper to share with a friend.

**Create a rainbow-shaped home.**

**Create a rainbow-shaped food item.**

Description: _____

_____

_____

_____

Description: _____

_____

_____

_____

**Create a rainbow-shaped toy.**

**Create a rainbow-shaped tool.**

Description: _____

_____

_____

_____

Description: _____

_____

_____

_____

 **Try This!** **Names, Please** Think of a name for each item that you drew.

# Deer Me!

**Read this comic and then answer the question below.**

**What do you think the farmer's idea could have been? List two ways to get the deer out of the farmer's field without hurting them.**

1. _____

_____

2. _____

_____

**Try This!** **Solutions Needed** Some animals, like deer, are in no danger of dying out. Other animals, in contrast, are in danger of becoming extinct. What creative approaches might scientists use to try to preserve endangered species? List as many ideas as you can.

# Magic Squares

**What's a lot older than TV and video games and just as interesting? Magic squares! The first magic square was created in China around the year 2,800 B.C. From China, the magic square spread to India, Japan, the Middle East, Africa, and finally to Europe and America.**

A magic square is an array of numbers arranged this way:
1. The square has the same number of rows and columns.
2. No number is used more than once.
3. The sum of every row, column, and diagonal is the same number.

Below are two magic squares that have been started for you. Complete each one by placing numbers between 1 and 9 in the squares so the sum of the rows and columns is 15.

| 8 |   | 6 |
|---|---|---|
|   | 5 | 7 |
| 4 | 9 |   |

| 4 |   | 2 |
|---|---|---|
|   | 5 |   |
|   |   | 6 |

Arrange the numbers 3, 6, 9, 12, 15, 18, 21, 24, and 27 in the squares so that the sums of all the rows, columns, and diagonals is 45.

| 18 |   |    |
|----|---|----|
|    |   |    |
|    |   | 12 |

Arrange the numbers 4, 5, 6, 7, 8, 9, 10, 11, and 12 in the squares so that the sums of all the rows, columns, and diagonals is 24.

|   |   |   |
|---|---|---|
|   | 8 |   |
|   |   |   |

💡 **Try This!**  **Make Magic**
Create a magic square of your own!

# All Mixed Up

**Salad is good and good for you, but the dressing never stays mixed. You always have to shake it before you pour it on your salad. Why don't the oil and vinegar stay mixed? Find out with this simple experiment.**

## Here's what you'll need:

1 tablespoon vinegar
2 tablespoons oil (corn oil or olive oil)
dash of salt
dash of pepper
dash of sugar
a clean glass jar with a cover
a fork or spoon
salad (lettuce, carrots, tomatoes, and so on)

## Here's what to do:

1. Put the salt, pepper, and sugar in the jar.
2. Add the vinegar and stir it all up.
3. Add the oil. Stir it all up.
4. Chill the salad dressing. What do you see?
5. Screw the lid on tightly. Shake the dressing. What happens? Why?

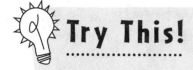 **Try This!** Have a Salad
Make a salad and use your dressing on it.

# A Yellow Submarine

**How do submarines dive under the water and rise to the surface again? Make your own submarine to find out.**

**Here's what you'll need:**

glass jar      large balloon      fresh lemon
scissors      rubber band      water

**Here's what to do:**

1. With the help of an adult, cut a piece of lemon peel into the shape of a submarine.

2. Fill the jar with water. Put the lemon peel submarine in the water.

3. Cut a circle from the balloon. Stretch it over the top of the jar. Hold the balloon in place with the rubber band.

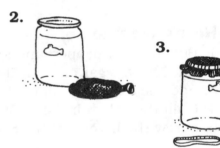

4. Press hard on the balloon. What happens to your submarine?

5. Take your finger off the balloon. What happens to your submarine now?

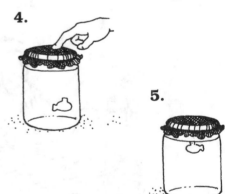

6. Can you explain why this happens? What does this tell you about how submarines dive under the water and rise to the surface again?

 **Try This!**    **Recording Observations** Take notes about your experiment in a science notebook.

# Invention Convention

Invite students to create and build their own fantastic inventions. Have each student begin by deciding on the function of his or her invention. Then have students fashion their inventions from commonplace materials such as cardboard boxes, paper, string, cardboard tubes, and found objects. When all the students have completed their work, have them write brief descriptions of their inventions' purposes and functions. Then encourage each inventor to share his or her invention with the class. If you like, you can award certificates for the most practical, the best designed, and the wackiest inventions!

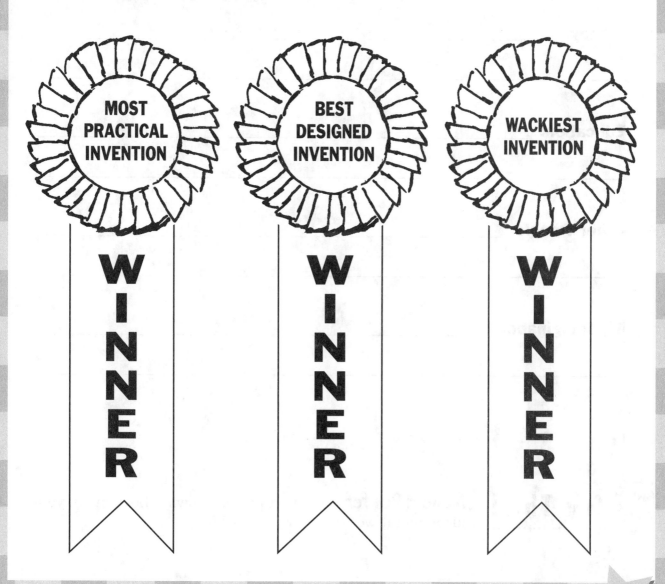

**Name** _____

# Change the World!

There are many problems facing America today.  Some of these include pollution, homelessness, and crime.  What do you think is the biggest problem our country faces?  How would you solve it?

**The largest problem in America today is:** _____

_____

**How would you use the following four means—money, education, other people, and your imagination—to solve the problem?**

**Money:** _____

_____

**Education:** _____

_____

**Other People:** _____

_____

**My Imagination:** _____

_____

 **Try This!**   **Make a Poster** Design a poster showing how one of your ideas might work.

# Answers

## Recognizing and Recalling Activities

### Trivia Trackdown, page 10
1. 64
2. Pluto
3. an elephant
4. the Kitty Hawk
5. Albany
6. teeth
7. Sandra Day O'Connor
8. Canada and Mexico
9. Dr. Seuss
10. one
11. John Adams
12. three
13. Kansas and Missouri
14. Casper
15. Erie, Ontario, Michigan, Huron, Superior
16. Leonardo da Vinci
17. water
18. six
19. four
20. two

### Recycled Words, page 13
1. eye       6. ship
2. land      7. rain
3. new       8. snow
4. road      9. play
5. run       10. egg

### What Am I?, page 14
1. hail          6. heart
2. haiku         7. hero
3. half          8. high
4. hamburger     9. history
5. hay fever     10. Holland

### Transformations, page 19
1. 3      2. 2      3. 2      4. 6      5. 5      6. 2

## Distinguishing and Visualizing Activities

### Within a Word, page 25
1. barbell        2. barn       3. barber
4. barrette       5. barge      6. wheelbarrow
7. barbed wire    8. barrel     9. bar graph

### Real Estate, page 26
1. 2      2. 5      3. 3      4. 9
5. 1      6. 4      7. 3      8. 4

### Tricky Twins, page 27
Single cats: row 1, first and third cat from the left; row 3, first cat from the left

### Stargazing, page 28

```
M N O R T H S T A R
I C R S W R U M N J
L H I S Y U U S E A
K A O T U L P A A Z
Y R N O O M O T R U
W L Q U A A Y U T Z
A E L O B R O R H O
Y S P W B S U N E V
```

### Triangle Challenge, page 29
13 triangles

### How Do You Hide an Elephant?, page 31

1. Go fis**h or se** e what we have to eat in the refrigerator.
2. **Be ar** tistic and paint a picture for me.
3. S **he n** eeds a new cover for her book.
4. To **m ice** d the cake for the birthday party.
5. **Do g** irls like soccer or baseball?
6. Ms. **Dee r** ead a book to the class.
7. What a big b **owl** of noodles you have!
8. Ho **p on y** our bicycle and let's go for a ride.
9. Jess took **a pe** ek into the package.
10. "S **lam b** am!" the ball hit the rim with a crash!
11. Jay did kic **k it ten** times in row.
12. Please have dinne **r at** my house on Monday.

### Magic Words, page 32

1. rose
2. sub
3. dad
4. ton
5. notes
6. plane
7. ten
8. owl
9. war
10. seal

### Anagram Adventure, page 33

1. read, dear
2. seat, eats
3. team, mate, tame
4. reap, pare
5. tales, least, steal
6. span, naps
7. nails, slain
8. race, care
9. laps, pals

## Following Directions and Classifying

### Wrong Rhymes, page 39

1. matter
2. got
3. lacked
4. furry
5. train
6. down
7. talk
8. light
9. lake
10. cheery
11. jump
12. run
13. taste
14. spill
15. boat
16. dead
17. sock
18. sooner
19. hike
20. bread

### Scrambled Sentences, page 43

I went to my doctor and I said, "Doctor, I broke my arm in three places." He said, "Well, stay out of those places."

### Get Set, page 47

Possible responses:

1. All the vowels make a set; all the consonants make another set.
2. The *jet, kite, glider, helicopter* make one set because they are all manufactured items that fly. The *robin, eagle, sparrow, hummingbird* make another set because they are all birds that fly.
3. Set #1 is green vegetables. Set #2 is yellow fruits. The intersection has fruits and vegetables that are both green and yellow.

### In Groups, page 48

Possible responses:

1. A kitten is not a wild animal.
2. A tack is not a tool.
3. Track is the only sport that does not use a ball.
4. A melon does not have a pit.
5. Albany is not a state.
6. A ruby is not a metal.
7. You cannot write with a ruler.
8. Drums are not wind instruments.
9. Every word but *arrive* means to leave.
10. A horse is not a baby animal.
11. You cannot read a radio.
12. A foot is not a part of a face.

### Prime Time Numbers, page 49

2, 3, 5, 7, 11, 13, 17, 19, 23, 29, 31, 37, 41, 43, 47, 53, 59, 61, 67, 71, 73, 79, 83, 89, 97

Try This! Answers can include 11, 13; 17, 19; 29, 31; 41, 43; 59, 61.

## Sequencing and Predicting

### Pressed for Time, page 54

| | |
|---|---|
| Pie-Eating Contest | 10:00–10:45 |
| Brass Band | 11:15–11:45 |
| Sack Race | 12:00–12:30 |
| Corn Shucking | 1:00–1:45 |

## Inferring and Drawing Conclusions

### Constant Confusion, page 70

1. Jessica
2. Judith
3. Justina
4. Jennifer
5. Jackie

### Shhh! page 71

2. ● is an *e*

3. ▲ is an *n*

4. ◆ is a *c*

5. ● is an *i*

6. ⬟ is an *l*

The password is *pencil*

**Q & A, page 72**

Possible responses:

1. maps, food, directions
2. The grill would be warm; there would be a pile of ashes.
3. The land was rocky, there was no water, it was cold and barren.
4. Ask the person to lift something heavy; look at the person's muscles.
5. He saw rice on the ground; there were happy people and white limousines outside the church.
6. Both are animals, both give products that people use, both live on farms.
7. Drop a rock into the hole and see how long it takes to hit the ground; yell down and listen to the echo; tie a rock on a string and lower it into the hole.
8. You saw trees and leaves moving; you saw clothing blowing on a wash line.
9. It's too cold, too hot, too rainy, too rocky, or too dry.
10. The "lights" could be people with flashlights, the eyes of an animal, or campfires.

**Make a Wish, page 73**

| denomination | amount | total |
| --- | --- | --- |
| pennies | 6 | 6¢ |
| nickels | 6 | 30¢ |
| dimes | 2 | 20¢ |
| **Total** | **14** | **56¢** |

# Evaluating

**Fact or Opinion?, page 83**

1. opinion
2. fact
3. opinion
4. fact
5. fact
6. opinion
7. fact
8. fact
9. fact
10. fact
11. opinion
12. fact
13. fact
14. opinion
15. fact
16. opinion
17. fact
18. opinion
19. fact
20. fact

**Twins?, page 85**

Possible responses:

| Objects | How Alike |
| --- | --- |
| 1. sweater/blanket | used for warmth; used as covers |
| 2. wind/water | natural forces; can be destructive; can be energy sources; can move objects |
| 3. fish/soap | go in water; float; slippery when wet |
| 4. puppy/baby | need love, food, and attention; cry when unhappy; cannot survive alone |
| 5. pencil/candle | long, thin shape; exterior material different from interior material; get shorter with use |
| 6. oatmeal/bread | eaten for breakfast; grains; need to be cooked before they can be eaten |
| 7. rain/tears | liquid; wet; transparent; associated with sadness |
| 8. lion/eagle | symbols of power; predators; hunted |
| 9. comb/saw | have pointed edges; teeth; held in your hands |
| 10. spring/youth | part of a cycle; new beginnings |

# Analyzing

**Puzzle Pattern, page 91**

1. The shaded square moved down one space.
2. The shaded square again moved down one space.
3. The shaded square moved to the right. It will move to the right again.

**What Does It Represent?, page 93**

Possible responses:

a dove: peace; an eagle: America, strength, power, victory; the American flag: America, democracy, freedom, equality; a red rose: love, passion; a fox: craftiness, slyness; an owl: wisdom; a wedding ring: marriage; a four-leaf clover: good luck

**Dare Dare, page 94**

1. forget it!
2. head over heels
3. upset stomach
4. four-wheel drive

117

### Flower Power, page 95

|  | Orange | Yellow | White | Total |
|---|---|---|---|---|
| Daffodils | 1 | 3 | 6 | 10 |
| Tulips | 6 | 0 | 4 | 10 |
| Totals | 7 | 3 | 10 | 20 |

### Odd Couples, page 96

Possible responses:

1. Both are the young of the species; both require care.
2. Both are machines that convert words into type; both need human operators.
3. Both are a means of communication; both can entertain.
4. Both can help the environment; both come out after rain.
5. Both are sources of energy; both can be dangerous.
6. Both use air; both entertain.
7. Both are times of hope and possibility; both are part of a cycle.
8. Both are odd numbers; both are prime.
9. Both live in the jungle; both are hunted.
10. Both are fruits; both are red.

### Divide and Conquer, page 97

1.

2.

3. Triangle cannot be divided into four equal pieces.

4.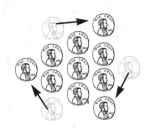

### Riddle Me This, page 98

| Joke | Answer |
|---|---|
| 1. What's easy to get into but hard to get out of? | Trouble |
| 2. Why did the man pour veggies all over the world? | He wanted peas on Earth. |
| 3. When is a car not a car? | When it turns into a driveway |
| 4. If 2 is company and 3 is a crowd, what's 4 and 5? | Nine |
| 5. How can you make a hamburger roll? | Take it up a hill and push it down. |
| 6. If I had 6 oranges in one hand and 8 in the other, what would I have? | Very big hands |
| 7. Why did the candle fall in love? | He met the perfect match. |
| 8. Where was the Declaration of Independence signed? | On the bottom |
| 9. Why do ducks fly south? | Because it's too far to walk |

### Amazing Analogies, page 99

Possible responses:

1. ocean
2. foot
3. square
4. dog
5. soil
6. Halloween
7. floors
8. snow
9. bunch
10. paints
11. watch
12. sour

### Puzzling Problems, page 100

1. Smash the tip against the table. The bottom of the egg will be flat and the egg will stand on end.
2. Stand in a doorway. Place a sheet of newspaper so half is on one side of the door and half is on the other. Close the door between the people.
3. The dentist was the boy's mother.
4.

5. Fill the five-quart bottle and pour as much as you can into the three-quart bottle. Now empty the three quarts. Then pour the remaining two quarts into the three-quart bottle. Fill the five quart bottle again. Use it to fill the three-quart bottle. There are already two quarts in the three-quart bottle, so it will take one more quart. Four quarts will be left in the five-quart bottle.

# Synthesizing

### Deer Me!, page 109

Possible responses:
1. Spray the plants with a repellent that does not harm them or the deer but makes the plants unappealing to the deer.
2. Have dogs patrol the area and scare off the deer.
3. Place food in another area to attract the deer to settle there.

Try This!: Clone duplicates of the animals now and freeze the animals' reproductive cells for duplication later.

### Magic Squares, page 110

| 8 | 1 | 6 |
|---|---|---|
| 3 | 5 | 7 |
| 4 | 9 | 2 |

| 4 | 9 | 2 |
|---|---|---|
| 3 | 5 | 7 |
| 8 | 1 | 6 |

Answers will vary. Here is one possible arrangement:

| 18 | 21 | 6 |
|----|----|---|
| 3 | 15 | 27 |
| 24 | 9 | 12 |

| 9 | 10 | 5 |
|---|----|---|
| 4 | 8 | 12 |
| 11 | 6 | 7 |

### All Mixed Up, page 111

The dressing will separate into layers, with the oil on the top and everything else on the bottom. This occurs because vinegar is mostly water and water and oil don't mix. Since oil is lighter than vinegar, it floats on the top. When the dressing is shaken, the layers disappear because the oil breaks into little drops, which are suspended in the vinegar for some time.

### A Yellow Submarine, page 112

When the student presses hard on the balloon, the submarine will sink. When the pressure is removed, the submarine will rise. This happens because air can be compressed into a smaller area, but water cannot. When pressure is applied to the balloon, the tiny bubbles of air in the lemon peel are compressed. This allows more water to enter the peel, which makes the submarine heavier, so it sinks a little. When the pressure is removed, the air expands again, expelling the water. This makes the submarine lighter so it rises again.

# Notes